BLAKE'S
English Guide

for primary students

Peter Clutterbuck

CONTENTS

CONTENTS

AUSTRALIAN CURRICULUM CORRELATIONS - YEAR 3

LANGUAGE	ELABORATIONS	ACELA	PAGE
Language variation and change			
Understand that languages have different written and visual communication systems, different oral traditions and different ways of constructing meaning	★ learning that a word can carry different weight in different cultural contexts, for example respect is due to some people and that stories can be passed on to teach us how to live appropriately	1475	3–4, 18–19, 38–9, 47, 51, 54, 62, 74–5, 86
Language for interaction			
Examine how evaluative language can be varied to be more or less forceful	★ exploring how modal verbs, for example 'must', 'might', or 'could' indicate degrees of certainty, command or obligation ★ distinguishing how choice of adverbs, nouns and verbs present different evaluations of characters in texts	1477	4, 10–13, 19, 42, 52, 56–9, 95–8
Text structure and organisation			
Understand how different types of texts vary in use of language choices, depending on their function and purpose, for example tense, mood and types of sentences	★ becoming familiar with typical structural stages and language features of various types of text, for example narratives, procedures, reports, reviews and expositions	1478	19, 34, 42–3, 53–4, 63, 84–5, 93–4, 95–8, 99
Understand that paragraphs are a key organisational feature of written texts	★ noticing how longer texts are organised into paragraphs, each beginning with a topic sentence or paragraph opener which predicts how the paragraph will develop and is then elaborated in various ways	1479	63
Know that word contractions are a feature of informal language and that apostrophes of contraction are used to signal missing letters	★ recognising both grammatically accurate and inaccurate usage of the apostrophe in everyday texts, such as in signs in the community and newspaper advertisements	1480	31, 76–7
Expressing and developing ideas			
Understand that a clause is a unit of meaning usually containing a subject and a verb and that these need to be in agreement	★ knowing that a clause is basically a group of words that contains a verb ★ knowing that, in terms of meaning, a basic clause represents: what is happening; who or what is participating, and the surrounding circumstances	1481	22, 42, 84–5
Understand that verbs represent different processes (doing, thinking, saying and relating) and that these processes are anchored in time through tense	★ identifying different types of verbs and the way they add meaning to a sentence ★ exploring action and saying verbs in narrative texts to show how they give information about what characters do and say	1482	19, 42–3, 64, 95–8
Learn extended and technical vocabulary and ways of expressing opinion including modal verbs and adverbs	★ exploring the use of sensing verbs and how they allow readers to know what characters think and feel ★ exploring the use of relating verbs in constructing definitions and descriptions ★ learning how time is represented through the tense of a verb and other structural, language and visual features	1484	10–13, 19, 38, 42–3, 52, 53, 93–4
Understand how to use sound–letter relationships and knowledge of spelling rules, compound words, prefixes, suffixes, morphemes and less common letter combinations, for example 'tion'	★ exploring examples of language which demonstrate a range of feelings and positions, and building a vocabulary to express judgments about characters or events, acknowledging that language and judgments might differ depending on the cultural context ★ using spelling strategies such as: phonological knowledge (for example diphthongs and other ambiguous vowel sounds in more complex words); three-letter clusters (for example 'thr', 'shr', 'squ'); visual knowledge (for example more complex single syllable homophones such as 'break/brake', 'ate/eight'); morphemic knowledge (for example inflectional endings in single syllable words, plural and past tense); generalisations (for example to make a word plural when it ends in 's', 'sh', 'ch' or 'z', add 'es')	1485	12, 26, 34, 44–6, 51, 54, 60, 68–9, 85, 86–9

LITERATURE		ACELT	
Responding to literature			
Develop criteria for establishing personal preferences for literature	★ building a conscious understanding of preference regarding topics and genres of personal interest (for example humorous short stories, school and family stories, mysteries, fantasy and quest, series books) ★ selecting and discussing favourite texts and explaining their reasons for assigning greater or lesser merit to particular texts or types of texts	1598	13, 38, 39, 51, 54, 62, 63, 93–4
Examining literature			
Discuss how language is used to describe the settings in texts, and explore how the settings shape the events and influence the mood of the narrative	★ identifying and discussing the use of descriptive adjectives ('in the middle of a vast, bare plain') to establish setting and atmosphere ('the castle loomed dark and forbidding') and to draw readers into events that follow ★ discussing the language used to describe the traits of characters in stories, their actions and motivations: 'Claire was so lonely; she desperately wanted a pet and she was afraid she would do anything, just anything, to have one to care for'	1599	5–10, 48, 65, 85
Discuss the nature and effects of some language devices used to enhance meaning and shape the reader's reaction, including rhythm and onomatopoeia in poetry and prose	★ identifying the effect of imagery in texts, for example the use of imagery related to nature in haiku poems ★ exploring how rhythm, onomatopoeia and alliteration give momentum to poetry and prose read aloud, and enhance enjoyment	1600	14, 18, 38, 48, 51, 59, 60–1, 66–7, 94

LITERATURE	ELABORATIONS	ACELT	PAGE
Creating literature			
Create imaginative texts based on characters, settings and events from students' own and other cultures using visual features, for example perspective, distance and angle	★ drawing on literary texts read, viewed and listened to for inspiration and ideas, appropriating language to create mood and characterisation ★ innovating on texts read, viewed and listened to by changing the point of view, revising an ending or creating a sequel	1601	48, 51, 65, 85, 93–4
Create texts that adapt language features and patterns encountered in literary texts, for example characterisation, rhyme, rhythm, mood, music, sound effects and dialogue	★ creating visual and multimodal texts based on Aboriginal and Torres Strait Islander or Asian literature, applying one or more visual elements to convey the intent of the original text ★ creating multimodal texts that combine visual images, sound effects, music and voice-overs to convey settings and events in a fantasy world	1791	14, 18, 33, 53–4, 60–1

LITERACY		ACELY	
Interpreting, analysing, evaluating			
Identify the audience and purpose of imaginative, informative and persuasive texts	★ identifying the author's point of view on a topic and key words and images that seem intended to persuade listeners, viewers or readers to agree with the view presented	1678	27, 38, 93–4
Read an increasing range of different types of texts by combining contextual, semantic, grammatical and phonic knowledge, using text processing strategies, for example monitoring, predicting, confirming, rereading, reading on and self-correcting	★ combining different types of knowledge (for example world knowledge, vocabulary, grammar, phonics) to make decisions about unknown words, reading on, reviewing and summarising meaning ★ analysing the way illustrations help to construct meaning and interpreting different types of illustrations and graphics ★ reading text types from a student's culture to enhance confidence in building reading strategies ★ reading aloud with fluency and intonation ★ reading a wider range of texts, including chapter books and informative texts, for pleasure	1679	27, 93–4
Use comprehension strategies to build literal and inferred meaning and begin to evaluate texts by drawing on a growing knowledge of context, text structures and language features	★ making connections between the text and student's own experience and other texts ★ making connections between the information in print and images ★ making predictions and asking and answering questions about the text drawing on knowledge of the topic, subject-specific vocabulary and experience of texts on the same topic ★ using text features and search tools to locate information in written and digital texts efficiently ★ determining important ideas, events or details in texts commenting on things learned or questions raised by reading, referring explicitly to the text for verification ★ making considered inferences taking into account topic knowledge or a character's likely actions and feelings	1680	27, 49
Creating texts			
Plan, draft and publish imaginative, informative and persuasive texts demonstrating increasing control over text structures and language features and selecting print, and multimodal elements appropriate to the audience and purpose	★ using print and digital resources to gather information about a topic ★ selecting appropriate text structure for a writing purpose and sequencing content for clarity and audience impact ★ using appropriate simple, compound and complex sentences to express and combine ideas ★ using vocabulary, including technical vocabulary, relevant to the text type and purpose, and appropriate sentence structures to express and combine ideas	1682	41, 63, 65, 93–4, 98
Reread and edit texts for meaning, appropriate structure, grammatical choices and punctuation	★ using glossaries, print and digital dictionaries and spell check to edit spelling, realising that spell check accuracy depends on understanding the word function, for example there/their; rain/reign	1683	42–3, 44–6, 75–82, 86–9

LANGUAGE	ELABORATIONS	ACELA	PAGE
Language variation and change Understand that Standard Australian English is one of many social dialects used in Australia, and that while it originated in England it has been influenced by many other languages	★ identifying words used in Standard Australian English that are derived from other languages, including Aboriginal and Torres Strait Islander languages, and determining if the original meaning is reflected in English usage, for example kangaroo, tsunami, typhoon, amok, orangutan ★ identifying commonly used words derived from other cultures	1487	3–4, 14–15, 18–19, 36–7, 39, 44, 90–1
Language for interaction Understand that social interactions influence the way people engage with ideas and respond to others for example when exploring and clarifying the ideas of others, summarising students' own views and reporting them to a larger group	★ recognising that we can use language differently with our friends and families, but that Standard Australian English is typically used in written school texts & more formal contexts ★ recognising that language is adjusted in different contexts, for example in degree of formality when moving between group discussions and presenting a group report ★ understanding how age, status, expertise and familiarity influence the ways in which we interact with people and how these codes and conventions vary across cultures ★ recognising the importance of using inclusive language	1488	24–5, 27, 31, 55, 86, 93–4, 98
Understand the differences between the language of opinion and feeling and the language of factual reporting or recording	★ identifying ways thinking verbs are used to express opinion, for example 'I think', 'I believe', and ways summary verbs are used to report findings, for example 'we concluded'	1489	27, 28, 38, 40, 41, 52, 53, 93–4, 95–6
Text structure and organisation Understand how texts vary in complexity and technicality depending on the approach to the topic, the purpose and the intended audience	★ becoming familiar with the typical stages and language features of such text types as simple narrative, procedure, simple persuasion texts and information reports	1490	27, 41, 51, 93–4, 99
Understand how texts are made cohesive through the use of linking devices including pronoun reference and text connectives	★ knowing how authors construct texts that are cohesive and coherent through the use of: pronouns that link back to something previously mentioned; determiners (for example 'this', 'that', 'these', 'those', 'the', 'his', 'their'); text connectives that create links between sentences (for example 'however', 'therefore', 'nevertheless', 'in addition', 'by contrast', 'in summary') ★ identifying how a topic is described throughout a text by tracking noun groups and pronouns ★ describing how texts connectives link sections of a text providing sequences through time (for example 'firstly', 'then', 'next', and 'finally')	1491	10–13, 29–30, 43, 63, 65, 69–72
Recognise how quotation marks are used in texts to signal dialogue, titles and reported speech	★ exploring texts to identify the use of quotation marks ★ experimenting with the use of quotation marks in students' own writing	1492	33, 34, 81–2
Expressing and developing ideas Understand that the meaning of sentences can be enriched through the use of noun and verb groups and prepositional phrases	★ creating richer, specific descriptions through the use of noun groups (eg in narrative texts, 'Their very old Siamese cat'; in reports, 'Its extremely high mountain ranges')	1493	42–3, 65, 69–70, 95–8
Investigate how quoted (direct) and reported (indirect) speech work in different types of text	★ investigating examples of quoted (direct) speech ('He said, "I'll go to the park today"') and reported (indirect) speech ('He told me he was going to the park today') and comparing similarities and differences	1494	3, 34, 48–9
Understand how adverbials (adverbs and prepositional phrases) work in different ways to provide circumstantial details about an activity	★ investigating in texts how adverbial phrases and clauses can add significance to an action, for example 'more desperately', 'he rose quietly and gingerly moved'	1495	10–13, 42–3, 65, 69–70
Explore the effect of choices when framing an image, placement of elements in the image, and salience on composition of still and moving images in a range of types of texts	★ examining visual and multimodal texts, building a vocabulary to describe visual elements and techniques such as framing, composition and visual point of view and beginning to understand how these choices impact on viewer response	1496	48
Incorporate new vocabulary from a range of sources into students' own texts including vocabulary encountered in research	★ building etymological knowledge about word origins (for example 'thermometer') and building vocabulary from research about technical and subject specific topics	1498	13, 36–7, 39, 50, 54, 58–9, 68–9, 83, 90–1
Understand how to use strategies for spelling words, including spelling rules, knowledge of morphemic word families, spelling generalisations, and letter combinations including double letters	★ using phonological knowledge (eg long vowel patterns in multi-syllabic words); consonant clusters (for example 'straight', 'throat', 'screen', 'squawk') ★ using visual knowledge (for example diphthongs in more complex words and other ambiguous vowel sounds, as in 'oy', 'oi', 'ou', 'ow', 'ould', 'u', 'ough', 'au', 'aw'); silent beginning patterns (for example 'gn' and 'kn') ★ applying generalisations, such as doubling (for example 'running'); 'e'-drop (for example 'hoping')	1779	12, 34, 51, 54, 60, 85, 86–9
Recognise homophones and know how to use context to identify correct spelling	★ using meaning and context when spelling words (for example when differentiating between homophones such as 'to', 'too', 'two')	1780	44–6

LITERATURE		ACELT	
Literature and context Make connections between the ways different authors may represent similar storylines, ideas and relationships	★ commenting on how authors have established setting and period in different cultures and times and the relevance of characters, actions and beliefs to their own time ★ comparing different authors' treatment of similar themes and text patterns, for example comparing fables and allegories from different cultures and quest novels by different authors	1602	13, 38, 39, 51
Responding to literature Use metalanguage to describe the effects of ideas, text structures and language features of literary texts	★ examining the author's description of a character's appearance, behaviour and speech and noting how the character's development is evident through his or her dialogue and changing relationships and the reactions of other characters to him or her ★ sharing views using appropriate metalanguage (for example 'The use of the adjectives in describing the character really helps to create images for the reader')	1604	5–13, 33, 34, 48, 65

LITERATURE	ELABORATIONS	ACELT	PAGE
Examining literature Discuss how authors and illustrators make stories exciting, moving and absorbing and hold readers' interest by using various techniques, for example character development and plot tension	★ examining the author's description of a character's appearance, behaviour and speech and noting how the character's development is evident through his or her dialogue and changing relationships and the reactions of other characters to him or her ★ defining spoonerisms, neologisms and puns and exploring how they are used by authors to create a sense of freshness, originality and playfulness	1605	5–13, 33, 34, 48, 65
Understand, interpret and experiment with a range of devices and deliberate word play in poetry and other literary texts, for example nonsense words, spoonerisms, neologisms and puns	★ discussing poetic language, including unusual adjectival use and how it engages us emotionally and brings to life the poet's subject matter (for example 'He grasps the crag with crooked hands'/wee timorous beastie)	1606	14, 18, 60–1, 63, 66–7, 82, 90, 94

LITERACY		ACELY	
Interacting with others Interpret ideas and information in spoken texts and listen for key points in order to carry out tasks and use information to share and extend ideas and information	★ making notes about a task, asking questions to clarify or follow up information, and seeking assistance if required ★ discussing levels of language – slang, colloquial (everyday) and formal language – and how their appropriateness changes with the situation and audience. Presenting ideas and opinions at levels of formality appropriate to the context and audience	1687	24, 86
Interpreting, analysing, evaluating Identify characteristic features used in imaginative, informative and persuasive texts to meet the purpose of the text	★ describing the language which authors use to create imaginary worlds; how textual features such as headings, subheadings, bold type and graphic organisers are used to order and present information, and how visual codes are used, for example those used in advertising to represent children and families so that viewers identify with them	1690	27, 93–4
Read different types of texts by combining contextual, semantic, grammatical and phonic knowledge using text processing strategies for example monitoring meaning, cross-checking and reviewing	★ reading new and different kinds of texts with the use of established word identification strategies, including knowledge of the topic and of text type together with self-monitoring strategies; including rereading, self questioning and pausing, and including self correction strategies such as confirming and cross-checking ★ reading aloud with fluency and expression ★ reading a wide range of different types of texts for pleasure	1691	27, 93–4
Use comprehension strategies to build literal and inferred meaning to expand content knowledge, integrating and linking ideas and analysing and evaluating	★ making connections between the text and students' own experience and other texts ★ making connections between information in print and images ★ building and using prior knowledge and vocabulary ★ finding specific literal information ★ asking and answering questions ★ creating mental images ★ finding the main idea of a text ★ inferring meaning from the ways communication occurs in digital environments including the interplay between words, images, and sounds ★ bringing subject and technical vocabulary and concept knowledge to new reading tasks, selecting and using texts for their pertinence to the task and the accuracy of their information	1692	27, 49
Creating texts Plan, draft and publish imaginative, informative and persuasive texts containing key information and supporting details for a widening range of audiences, demonstrating increasing control over text structures and language features	★ using research from print and digital resources to gather ideas, integrating information from a range of sources; selecting text structure and planning how to group ideas into paragraphs to sequence content, and choosing vocabulary to suit topic and communication purpose ★ using appropriate simple, compound and complex sentences to express and combine ideas ★ using grammatical features effectively including different types of verbs, adverbials and noun groups for lengthier descriptions	1694	5–13, 22, 63, 84–5, 95–8
Reread and edit for meaning by adding, deleting or moving words or word groups to improve content and structure	★ revising written texts: editing for grammatical and spelling accuracy and clarity of the text, to improve the connection between ideas and overall flow of the piece	1695	42–3, 75–82, 86–9

LANGUAGE	ELABORATIONS	ACELA	PAGE
Language variation and change			
Understand that the pronunciation, spelling and meanings of words have histories and change over time	★ recognising that a knowledge of word origins is not only interesting in its own right, but that it extends students' knowledge of vocabulary and spelling	1500	3–4, 14–15, 18–19, 36–7, 44, 53, 60–1, 83, 90–1
Language for interaction			
Understand that patterns of language interaction vary across social contexts and types of texts and that they help to signal social roles and relationships	★ identifying ways in which cultures differ in making and responding to common requests, for example periods of silence, degrees of formality	1501	18–19
Understand how to move beyond making bare assertions and take account of differing perspectives and points of view	★ recognising that a bare assertion (for example 'It's the best film this year') often needs to be tempered by: using the impersonal 'it' to distance oneself (for example 'It could be that it is the best film this year'); recruiting anonymous support (for example 'It is generally agreed that it is the best film this year'); indicating a general source of the opinion (for example 'Most critics agree that it is the best film this year'); specifying the source of the opinion (for example 'David and Margaret both agree that it is the best film this year'), and reflecting on the effect of these different choices	1502	27, 38, 49, 50, 52, 93–4
Text structure and organisation			
Understand how texts vary in purpose, structure and topic as well as the degree of formality	★ becoming familiar with the typical states and language features of such text types as narrative, procedure, exposition, explanation, discussion and informative text and how they can be composed and presented in written, digital and multimedia forms	1504	27, 41, 51, 93–4, 99
Understand that the starting point of a sentence gives prominence to the message in the text and allows for prediction of how the text will unfold	★ observing how writers use the beginning of a sentence to signal to the reader how the text is developing (for example 'Snakes are reptiles. They have scales and no legs. Many snakes are poisonous. However, in Australia they are protected.')	1505	84–5, 99
Understand how possession is signalled through apostrophes of possession for common and proper nouns	★ examining how conventions of punctuation are used in written and digitally composed lists and learning that in Standard Australian English it is not necessary to add another 's' to the end of a plural noun to indicated possession ('James' house'/ 'my parents' car')	1506	76–7
Expressing and developing ideas			
Understand the difference between main and subordinate clauses and how these can be combined to create complex sentences through subordinating conjunctions to develop and expand ideas	★ knowing that the function of complex sentences is to make connections between ideas, such as: to provide a reason (for example 'He jumped up because the bell rang.'); to state a purpose (eg 'She raced home in order to confront her brother.'); to express a condition (for example 'It will break if you push it.'); to make a concession (for example 'She went to work even though she was not feeling well.'); to link two idea in terms of various time relations (for example 'Nero fiddled while Rome burned.')	1507	2, 29–30
Understand how noun and adjective groups can be expanded in a variety of ways to provide a fuller description of the person, thing or idea	★ learning how to expand a description by combining a related set of nouns and adjectives – 'Two old brown cattle dogs sat on the ruined front veranda of the deserted house'	1508	5–10, 56, 65
Understand the use of vocabulary to express greater precision of meaning, and know that words can have different meanings in different contexts	★ moving from general, 'all-purpose' words, for example 'cut' to more specific words for example 'slice', 'dice', 'fillet', 'segment'	1512	3, 98
Understand how to use banks of known words as well as word origins, prefixes, suffixes and morphemes to learn and spell new words Recognise uncommon plurals, for example 'foci'	★ learning that many complex words were originally hyphenated but have become 'prefixed' as in 'uncommon', 'renew', 'email' and 'refine' ★ talking about how suffixes change over time and new forms are invented to reflect changing attitudes to gender, for example 'policewoman', 'salesperson'; 'air hostess' / 'steward' or 'flight attendant'	1513	40, 54, 68–9, 80, 83, 90–1
Recognise uncommon plurals, for example 'foci'	★ using knowledge of word origins and roots and related words to interpret and spell unfamiliar words, and learning how these roots impact on plurals	1514	60
LITERATURE		**ACELT**	
Responding to literature			
Use metalanguage to describe the effects of ideas, text structures and language features on particular audiences	★ orally, in writing or using digital media, giving a considered interpretation and opinion about a literary text, recognising that a student's view may not be shared by others and that others have equal claims to divergent views	1795	27, 50

AUSTRALIAN CURRICULUM CORRELATIONS - YEAR 5 continued

LITERATURE	ELABORATIONS	ACELT	PAGE
Examining literature			
Recognise that ideas in literary texts can be conveyed from different view points, which can lead to different kinds of interpretations and responses	★ identifying the narrative voice (the person or entity through whom the audience experiences the story) in a literary work, discussing the impact of first person narration on empathy and engagement	1610	27, 93–4
Understand, interpret and experiment with sound devices and imagery, including simile, metaphor and personification, in narratives, shape poetry, songs, anthems and odes	★ discussing how figurative language including simile and metaphor can make use of a comparison between different things, for example 'My love is like a red, red rose'; 'Tyger! Tyger! Burning bright, In the forests of the night'; and how by appealing to the imagination, it provides new ways of looking at the world ★ investigating the qualities of contemporary protest songs for example those about indigenous peoples or those about the environment	1611	48, 51, 65, 66–7, 85
Creating literature			
Create literary texts that experiment with structures, ideas and stylistic features of selected authors	★ drawing upon fiction elements in a range of model texts – for example main idea, characterisation, setting (time and place), narrative point of view; and devices, for example figurative language (simile, metaphor, personification), as well as non-verbal conventions in digital and screen texts – in order to experiment with new, creative ways of communicating ideas, experiences and stories in literary texts	1798	38, 51, 65, 85

LITERACY		ACELY	
Texts in context			
Show how ideas and points of view in texts are conveyed through the use of vocabulary, including idiomatic expressions, objective and subjective language, and that these can change according to context	★ identifying the narrative voice (the person or entity through whom the audience experiences the story) in a literary work, discussing the impact of first person narration on empathy and engagement	1698	20, 47, 93–4
Interpreting, analysing, evaluating			
Navigate and read texts for specific purposes applying appropriate text processing strategies, for example predicting and confirming, monitoring meaning, skimming and scanning	★ bringing subject and technical vocabulary and concept knowledge to new reading tasks ★ electing and using texts for their pertinence to the task and the accuracy of their information ★ using word identification, self-monitoring and self-correcting strategies to access material on less familiar topics, skimming and scanning to check the pertinence of particular information to students' topic and task ★ reading a wide range of imaginative, informative and persuasive texts for pleasure and to find and use information	1702	27
Use comprehension strategies to interpret and analyse information, integrating and linking ideas from a variety of print and digital sources	★ using research skills including identifying research purpose, locating texts, gathering and organising information, evaluating its relative value, and the accuracy and currency of print and digital sources and summarising information from several sources	1703	27
Creating texts			
Plan, draft and publish imaginative, informative and persuasive print and multimodal texts, choosing text structures, language features, images and sound appropriate to purpose and audience	★ using research from print and digital resources to gather and organise information for writing ★ selecting and appropriate text structure for the writing purpose and sequencing content according to that text structure, introducing the topic, and grouping related information in well-sequenced paragraphs with a concluding statement ★ using vocabulary, including technical vocabulary, appropriate to the type of text and purpose. Using appropriate grammatical features, including more complex sentences and relevant verb tense, pronoun reference, adverbials and noun groups for lengthier descriptions	1704	50, 63, 84–5, 93–4

LANGUAGE	ELABORATIONS	ACELA	PAGE
Language variation and change			
Understand that different social and geographical dialects or accents are used in Australia in addition to Standard Australian English	★ recognising that there are more than 150 Aboriginal languages and two Torres Strait Islander languages and that they relation to geographic areas in Australia ★ recognising that all languages and dialects are of equal value, although we use different ones in different contexts, for example the use of Standard Australian English, Aboriginal English and forms of Creole used by some Torres Strait Islander groups and some of Australia's neighbours	1515	3–4, 18–19
Language for interaction			
Understand the uses of objective and subjective language and bias	★ understanding when it is appropriate to share feelings and opinions (for example in a personal recount) and when it is appropriate to remain more objective (for example in a factual recount) ★ differentiation between reporting the facts (for example in a news story) and providing commentary (for example in an editorial)	1517	20, 50, 53–4
Text structure and organisation			
Understand that cohesive links can be made in texts by omitting or replacing words	★ noting how writers often leave out words that have already been mentioned (for example 'Tina ate three apples and Simon ate two [apples].') ★ noting how writers often substitute a general word for a more specific word already mentioned, thus creating a cohesive link between the words (for example 'Look at those apples. Can I have one?') ★ recognising how cohesion can be developed through repeating key words or by using synonyms or antonyms ★ observing how relationships between concepts can be represented visually through similarity, contrast, juxtaposition, repetition, class–subclass diagrams, part–whole diagrams, cause and effect figures, visual continuities and discontinuities	1520	17, 91–2
Understand the used of commas to separate clauses	★ identifying different uses of commas in texts	1521	78–9
Expressing and developing ideas			
Investigating how clauses can be combined in a variety of ways to elaborate, extend or explain ideas	★ knowing that a complex sentence typically consists of an independent clause and a dependent clause connected by a subordinating conjunction (for example 'because', 'when', 'after', 'if', 'while', 'although'). Note: Dependent clauses of time, purpose, reason, concession, condition and so on are referred to as adverbial clauses ★ knowing that the function of complex sentences is to make connections between ideas, such as: to provide a reason (for example 'He jumped up because the bell rang'); to state a purpose (for example 'She raced home in order to confront her brother'); to express a condition (for example 'It will break if you push it'); to make a concession (for example 'She went to work even though she was not feeling well'); to link two ideas in terms of various time relations (for example 'Nero fiddled while Rome burned')	1522	22, 29–30, 84–5
Understand how ideas can be expanded and sharpened through careful choice of verbs, elaborated tenses and a range of adverbials	★ knowing that verbs often represent actions and that the choice of more expressive verbs makes an action more vivid (for example 'She ate her lunch' compared to 'She gobbled up her lunch')	1523	10–13, 64, 95–8
Investigate how vocabulary choices, including evaluative language, can express shades of meaning, feeling and opinion	★ identifying (for example from reviews) the ways in which evaluative language is used to assess the qualities of the various aspects of the work in question	1525	14, 38
Understand how to use banks of known words, word origins, base words, suffixes and prefixes, morphemes, spelling patterns and generalisations to learn and spell new words, for example technical words and words adopted from other languages	★ adopting a range of spelling strategies to recall and attempt to spell new words ★ using a dictionary to correct students' own spelling	1526	13, 33, 51, 54, 60, 68–9, 83, 86–9, 90–1
LITERATURE		ACELT	PAGE
Responding to literature			
Identify and explain how choices in language, for example modality, emphasis, repetition and metaphor, influence personal response to different texts	★ noting how degrees of possibility are opened up through the use of modal auxiliaries (for example 'It may be a solution'; 'It could be a solution') as well as through other resources, such as adverbs (for example 'It's possibly/probably/certainly a solution'); adjectives (for example 'It's a possible/probable/certain solution'); and nouns (for example 'It's a possibility/probability').	1615	5–13, 19, 51, 52, 53, 56–9

LITERATURE	ELABORATIONS	ACELT	PAGE
Creating literature			
Experiment with text structures and language features and their effects in creating literary texts, for example using imagery, sentence variation and metaphor	★ selecting and using sensory language to convey a vivid picture of places, feelings and events in a semi-structured verse form	1800	48, 51, 84–5, 93–4

LITERACY		ACELY	
Interacting with others		1709	27
Participate in and contribute to discussions, clarifying and integrating ideas, developing and supporting arguments, sharing and evaluating information, experiences and opinions	★ using strategies, for example pausing, questioning, rephrasing, repeating, summarising, reviewing and clarification ★ exploring personal reasons for acceptance or rejection of opinions offered and linking the reasons to the way our cultural experiences can affect our responses ★ recognising that closed questions ask for precise responses, while open questions prompt a speaker to provide more information		
Plan, rehearse and deliver presentations, selecting and sequencing appropriate content and multimodal elements for defined audiences and purposes, making appropriate choices for modality and emphasis	★ using technologies to prepare collaboratively a humorous, dynamic group view on a debatable topic, such as 'Kids should be able to read and view what they like', to be presented to teachers and parents	1710	19, 52
Interpreting, analysing and evaluating			
Use comprehension strategies to interpret and analyse information and ideas, comparing content from a variety of textual sources, including media and digital texts	★ making connections between the text and students' own experiences or other texts ★ making connections between information in print and images ★ finding specific literal information ★ using prior knowledge and textual information to make inferences and predictions ★ asking and answering questions ★ finding the main idea of a text ★ summarising a text or part of a text	1713	27
Analyse strategies authors use to influence readers **Creating texts**	★ identify how authors use language to position the reader and give reasons	1801	94
Plan, draft and publish imaginative, informative and persuasive texts, choosing and experimenting with text structures, language features, images and digital resources appropriate to purpose and audience	★ creating informative texts for two different audiences, such as a visiting academic and a Year 3 class, that explore an aspect of biodiversity ★ using rhetorical devices, images, surprise techniques and juxtaposition of people and ideas, and modal verbs and modal auxiliaries to enhance the persuasive nature of a text, recognising and exploiting audience susceptibilities	1714	19, 52, 93–4

HOW TO USE THIS BOOK

Blake's English Guide will provide you with the tools you need to use the English language – both written and spoken – correctly. It will help you gain knowledge about the spelling, grammar and punctuation rules of English, as well as those tricky parts of speech that are exceptions to the rules.

The concepts are arranged alphabetically and are thoroughly cross-referenced. Each entry contains a simple, concise definition as well as easily understood examples of usage. Reference lists are included under relevant headings, to provide students with plenty of easy-to-find examples.

The **TRY THIS** activities throughout the Guide allow students to consolidate and test their new knowledge.

Australian Curriculum correlation charts have been provided to enable teachers to easily program this Guide into their daily English lessons.

Both teachers and students will find Blake's English Guide invaluable in developing classroom activities and ensuring the basic areas of English are fully understood. Teachers and students will find the book an extensive and useful guide in the classroom and a valuable source of information to support their studies.

ABOUT THE AUTHOR

Peter Clutterbuck has written many best-selling English resources for primary schools. Blake's English Guide is the culmination of his years of experience teaching English, and his vast knowledge if its grammar, punctuation and usage.

ABBREVIATIONS

An abbreviation is a shortened form of a word or phrase. It saves time and space when writing.

There are different types of abbreviations:

- Some abbreviations are always substituted for the longer form. Examples: *Mr – Mister; Mrs – Mistress; am – ante meridiem; pm – post meridiem*

- Abbreviations are often used for titles, academic degrees, organisations, scientific words and measurements. Examples*: BA – Bachelor of Arts; Dr – Doctor; AFL – Australian Football League; CD-ROM – compact disc – read-only medium; cm – centimetres*

- Contractions abbreviate two words commonly used together. Examples*: can't – cannot; won't – will not; should've – should have*

- Some long or outdated words are always abbreviated in modern English. Examples*: bus – omnibus; budgie – budgerigar; email – electronic mail; DVD – digital versatile disc*

- Abbreviations of letters and numbers are used in text messaging. Examples*: SMS – short message service; ASAP – as soon as possible; CU L8R – see you later; LOL – laugh out loud*

Write abbreviations for: Liquid Petroleum Gas, Kilogram, Grievous Bodily Harm, Eastern Standard Time, Example

ABORIGINAL LANGUAGE

There were once hundreds of Indigenous languages spoken among the Australian Aboriginal people. Each clan or tribe had its own language and regional dialects.

Today there are fewer than 20 of these languages commonly spoken, but the names of many places in Australia have Aboriginal origins. For example, the South Australian rocket range and weapons testing site was named *Woomera*, which is an Aboriginal word meaning throwing stick.

Other examples include *Kyabram* (Vic) means dense forest; *Grong Grong* (NSW) is a bad camping ground; *Berriwillock* (Vic) means birds eating berries; and *Kununarra* (WA) means big water.

TRY THIS

These place names originated from the languages of the local Aboriginal people. Research what each name means: *Berrigan* (NSW), *Dunedoo* (NSW), *Omeo* (Vic), *Maralinga* (SA), *Murrumba* (Qld), *Dungog* (NSW), *Echuca* (Vic), *Popanyinning* (WA).

ABSOLUTE WORDS

Some words in English are complete in themselves. They cannot be more or less.

Example:

One of the dogs is **dead**.	Yes
One of the dogs is **more dead**.	No

Other absolute words include:

correct   final   perfect   unique   alive

ACRONYMS

Acronyms are a type of abbreviation. They are words formed by combining the initial (first) letters of a group of words.

Examples:

PIN – Personal Identification Number

LASER – Light Amplification by Stimulated Emission of Radiation

SCUBA – Self-Contained Underwater Breathing Apparatus

Find out what these acronyms stand for:

ANZAC, NASA, ATM, RADAR, ALCOA, AIDS

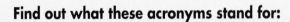

ADAGES

An adage is a wise saying that has been in use for many years.

Examples:

You must walk the walk before you can talk the talk.

There are two ways to get to the top of an oak tree – you can climb it or sit on an acorn.

An adage is an old saying, so don't ever say, **the old adage**. We know it is old

ADJECTIVES

Adjectives are words or phrases that tell us more about nouns or pronouns by describing them, adding detail or refining their meaning. Adjectives can add meaning and interest to sentences. A completely different picture can be produced by changing the adjectives in a sentence.

Examples:

*The **resentful** girl showed the **cranky** lady the way.*
*The **kind** girl showed the **old** lady the way.*
*The **savage** dog chased the **frightened** boy.*
*The **playful** dog chased the **laughing** boy.*

Some adjectives have become meaningless through overuse, such as a *nice* boy and a *good* story. Avoid such words in your writing and choose more expressive adjectives.

Examples:

*a **well-mannered** boy*   *an **exciting** story*

An adjective can come before or after the noun it is describing. However, you cannot put an adjective before a pronoun, it must go after.

Examples:

*The **big**, **black** dog.*   *They are **lazy**.*
*The dog was **big** and **black**.*   *It is **hot**.*

There are many types of adjectives. You should be familiar with the following types of adjectives and their uses.

Descriptive adjectives are the most common. They are used to describe the quality of a noun or pronoun.

Examples: *new   old   beautiful   ugly   big   small*

A

Number adjectives are used to show the number of things or the numerical order of things.

Examples:

Cardinal: **two** horses   **ten** fingers

Ordinal: the **first** in the queue   the **second** month

Indefinite adjectives are also used to refer to number but they do not tell us the exact number.

Examples: **Some** boys carried the tent.

Much fuss was made over the new baby.

Few suggestions were received.

Many cars were held up in the traffic jam.

Verbal adjectives have both a verb and an adjective function.

Examples: a **walking** stick   the **crashing** waves

smiling eyes   a **moving** poem

Adjectives of degree can change their form to indicate degrees of comparison of the qualities of people and things.

The three degrees are:

Positive degree – This is the regular form of the adjective.

Examples: a **sweet** lolly   a **muddy** boy   a **beautiful** rose

Comparative degree – This is used when we compare two people or things. We usually add **er** to the adjective, but for some words we put **more** in front of the adjective.

Examples: a **sweeter** lolly   a **muddier** boy   a **more beautiful** rose

Superlative degree – This is the highest degree and is used when we compare more than two people or things. It is made by adding **est** to the adjective or putting **most** in front of the adjective.

Examples: the **sweetest** lolly   the **muddiest** boy   the **most beautiful** rose

Things to remember:

- Some adjectives add **er** or **est** without any change to their spelling.
  Examples: *tall*   *taller*   *tallest*

- Adjectives that end in **e** drop the **e** when adding **er** or **est**.
  Examples: *large*   *larger*   *largest*

- If the adjective ends in **y** the **y** is changed to **i** before adding **er** or **est**.
  Examples: *heavy*   *heavier*   *heaviest*

- Some adjectives double the last letter before adding **er** or **est**.
  Examples: *big*   *bigger*   *biggest*

- Adjectives of three syllables or more (and even some of two syllables) have more before them for the comparative degree and most before them for the superlative degree.
  Examples: *honest*   *more honest*   *most honest*
  　　　　　　exciting   *more exciting*   *most exciting*

- Some adjectives only have a positive degree. For example, a thing can only be dead, it cannot be more dead.
  Examples: *full*   *empty*   *alive*   *perfect*   *correct*

- Some adjectives change their form for the different degrees.
  Examples: *bad, worse, worst*   *good, better, best*
  　　　　　　　　　　many, more, most

To recognise an adjective, ask questions such as:
What kind of?   How many?   Which?

Examples:
The old cars were demolished.
What kind of cars?   *old* (descriptive adjective)

Six flowers were in the glass vase.
How many flowers?   *six* (number adjective)
What kind of vase?   *glass* (descriptive adjective)

The younger girls are going swimming.
Which girls?   *younger* (adjective of degree)

Proper adjectives

These are formed from **Proper Nouns**.

Example: A wine from *Italy* (N) = An *Italian* (PA) wine.

Proper Adjectives

America	*American*	France	*French*	Mexico	*Mexican*
Australia	*Australian*	Germany	*German*	Morocco	*Moroccan*
Belgium	*Belgian*	Greece	*Greek*	Norway	*Norwegian*
Brazil	*Brazilian*	Iceland	*Icelandic*	Pakistan	*Pakistani*
Britain	*British*	India	*Indian*	Russia	*Russian*
Canada	*Canadian*	Iraq	*Iraqi*	Spain	*Spanish*
China	*Chinese*	Ireland	*Irish*	Sweden	*Swedish*
Denmark	*Danish*	Israel	*Israeli*	Thailand	*Thai*
Egypt	*Egyptian*	Italy	*Italian*	Tibet	*Tibetan*
Finland	*Finnish*	Japan	*Japanese*	Turkey	*Turkish*

Descriptive Adjectives

amazing	disobedient	gruesome	pink
annoying	dry	hollow	polluted
auburn	easy	immense	rich
beautiful	elegant	khaki	scarlet
blue	enormous	large	scorched
bright	exciting	loud	secluded
dangerous	filthy	marvellous	violent
deserted	fresh	mauve	violet
desolate	friendly	narrow	wrinkly
dirty	gorgeous	naughty	yellow
disgusting	green	occasional	young

Demonstrative Adjectives	Number Adjectives	Indefinite Adjectives
such	**cardinal:**	all
that	hundred	any
these	two	few
this	**ordinal:**	little
those	fifth	many
	second	much
	seventh	several
	eighth	some
	third	most
	ten	
	twelve	

Adjectives from nouns

Adjectives can be formed from nouns. The process of forming nouns from other parts of speech is called **nominalisation**.

NOUN	ADJECTIVE	NOUN	ADJECTIVE	NOUN	ADJECTIVE
accident	accidental	faith	faithful	muscle	muscular
advantage	advantageous	fame	famous	music	musical
adventure	adventurous	fashion	fashionable	mystery	mysterious
affection	affectionate	fault	faulty	nation	national
ancestor	ancestral	favour	favourite	nature	natural
angel	angelic	fire	fiery	noise	noisy
anger	angry	five	fifth	nonsense	nonsensical
anxiety	anxious	fool	foolish	occasion	occasional
athlete	athletic	fortune	fortunate	ocean	oceanic
autumn	autumnal	fraud	fraudulent	ornament	ornamental
beauty	beautiful	friend	friendly	peril	perilous
boy	boyish	fur	furry	person	personal
caution	cautious	fury	furious	picture	picturesque
centre	central	giant	gigantic	poison	poisonous
charity	charitable	girl	girlish	rebellion	rebellious
child	childish	gold	golden	region	regional
choir	choral	grace	graceful	response	responsible
circle	circular	grief	grievous	school	scholastic
colony	colonial	haste	hasty	sense	sensible
comfort	comfortable	hero	heroic	service	serviceable
continent	continental	humour	humorous	shower	showery
courage	courageous	industry	industrial	skill	skilful
coward	cowardly	influence	influential	star	starry
craft	crafty	injury	injurious	sun	sunny
credit	creditable	labour	laborious	suspicion	suspicious
crime	criminal	luxury	luxurious	sympathy	sympathetic
custom	customary	man	manly	tempest	tempestuous
danger	dangerous	marvel	marvellous	terror	terrible
deceit	deceitful	melody	melodious	triangle	triangular
disaster	disastrous	mercy	merciful	value	valuable
economy	economical	metal	metallic	victory	victorious
effect	effective	method	methodical	vigour	vigorous
energy	energetic	miracle	miraculous	volcano	volcanic
expense	expensive	mischief	mischievous	water	watery
expression	expressive	misery	miserable	winter	wintry
fable	fabulous	mountain	mountainous	wool	woollen

BLAKE'S ENGLISH GUIDE

A

What to Avoid when Using Adjectives

- Avoid using the **superlative degree** when the **comparative degree** is required.

  Wrong: *This book is the **best** of the two.*

  Right: *This book is the **better** of the two.*

- Do not use **less** instead of **fewer**.

  Wrong: *Ann made **less** mistakes than Diana.*

  Right: *Ann made **fewer** mistakes than Diana.*

  Less is used for a **quantity**.

  Examples: *less butter, less fruit, less money*

  Fewer is used for **numbers of things**.

  Examples: *fewer cows, fewer parties, fewer headaches*

- Avoid using **worse** for **worst**.

  Wrong: *Brendan is the **worse** writer in the class.*

  Right: *Brendan is the **worst** writer in the class.*

- Avoid using **more** with an adjective which forms its comparative degree by adding **er**.

  Wrong: *It is **more cheaper** to travel by road.*

  Right: *It is **cheaper** to travel by road.*

- Use **elder** and **eldest** for people, usually those of the same family.

  Examples:

  *Mr Payne's **elder** daughter is engaged.* (two daughters)

  *Mary is Mr Benn's **eldest** daughter.* (more than two)

- **Older** and **oldest** are used for things and unrelated persons.

  Examples: *This is the **oldest** castle in the country.*

  *George is the **oldest** inhabitant in the village.*

ADVERBS

An adverb is a word that adds meaning to a verb, an adjective or another adverb. There are many types of adverbs. You should be familiar with the following types of adverbs and their uses.

Adverbs of place are used to show where something happens.

Example: *I told him to come **here**.*

Other examples: *above   behind   below   upstairs*

outside   near   everywhere

Adverbs of time are used to show when or for how long something is happening.

Example: *He played **yesterday**.*

Other examples: *soon   later   tomorrow   today*
often   seldom   never   already   now   then

Adverbs of manner are used to show how something happens.

Example: *The child cried **loudly**.*

Other examples: *quietly   furiously   helpfully   softly*
gently   noisily

Interrogative adverbs ask questions.

Example: ***How** are you?*

Other examples: *when   whence   where   whither   why*

Negative adverbs make sentences negative. They are often written as contractions.

Examples: *He is **not** coming. I **don't** agree.*

Other examples: *never   hardly   didn't   can't*
won't   barely

Affirmative adverbs give sentences a positive feel or show agreement.

Example: *I will **certainly** be there.*

Other examples: *surely   undoubtedly   always   indeed*

Modal adverbs show agreement or express doubt.

Examples: *perhaps   possibly   probably   likely*
extremely   very   always

Adverbs of degree Like adjectives, adverbs can change their form to indicate degrees of comparison. The three degrees are:

- **Positive degree**: This refers to one person or thing.
  Example: *Tom tries **hard**.*
- **Comparative degree**: This compares two people or things.
  Example: *Tom tries **harder** than Ben.*
- **Superlative degree**: This compares more than two people or things.
  Example: *Of the three children, Tom tries the **hardest**.*

A

Things to remember:

- Adverbs of one syllable, add **er** and **est** to form the comparative and superlative.

  Examples: *hard*   *harder*   *hardest*

- Adverbs that end in **ly** have *more* and *most* placed before them to form the comparative and superlative degree.

  Examples: *carefully*   *more carefully*   *most carefully*

- Some adverbs are irregular.

  Examples: *badly*   *worse*   *worst*
  well   *better*   *best*
  much   *more*   *most*

- Some adverbs look like adjectives. You can tell they are adverbs if they add meaning to verbs, adjectives and other adverbs. If they add meaning to a noun, they are adjectives.

Adverbs from adjectives

Adverbs can be formed from adjectives by adding **ly** or just **y** but spelling changes are often needed.

No change	Change 'y' to 'i'	Drop 'e'	No change
cleverly	heartily	humbly	gratefully
sweetly	hungrily	nobly	thankfully
quickly	angrily	sensibly	hopefully
cheaply	noisily	gently	carefully
plainly	luckily	simply	truthfully
distinctly	steadily	miserably	skilfully
suddenly	shabbily	comfortably	mentally
poorly	wearily	idly	accidentally
fairly	heavily	horribly	brutally
proudly	clumsily	feebly	equally
bravely	merrily	possibly	loyally
anxiously	easily	truly	annually
gladly	haughtily	suitably	scornfully
patiently	lazily	terribly	fatally
willingly	prettily	probably	practically

Note that the **l** is not dropped when **ly** is added to adjectives ending with **ful**.

Adverbs of Place	Adverbs of Time	Adverbs of Manner	Interrogative Adverbs	Modal Adverbs
above	already	anxiously	how	definitely
behind	immediately	carefully	where	extremely
below	instantly	desperately	whither	often
downstairs	late	furiously	why	perhaps
elsewhere	lately	helpfully		possibly
everywhere	meanwhile	jauntily		probably
here	never	loudly		very
inside	now	nervously	**Negative Adverbs**	
near	often	noisily		
nowhere	presently	powerfully	hardly	
outside	recently	quietly	never	
somewhere	seldom	rapidly	not	
upstairs	shortly	skilfully	not at all	
within	soon	so	rarely	
yonder	then	tearfully	scarcely	
	today	trustingly	seldom	
	yesterday	urgently		
	yet	vigorously		
		well		

AFFIXES

An affix is a syllable added to a root or base word.

There are two types of affixes: **prefixes** and **suffixes**.

- A prefix is an addition to the front of the base word, which usually changes the word to one of opposite meaning. *(See Prefixes)*

- A suffix is an addition to the end of a word, which usually changes the part of speech. *(See Suffixes)*

ALLEGORY

An allegory is a story that has a symbolic meaning.
The characters in an allegory represent certain qualities.

An allegory can be poetry or prose and acts as an extended metaphor or parable. For example, *The Pilgrim's Progress* (1678) by John Bunyan is a famous English allegory in which the pilgrim's journey stands for the journey of life itself. *The Chronicles of Narnia* by C. S. Lewis can also be read as an allegory for the life of Jesus Christ, and the battle of good versus evil.

ALLITERATION

Alliteration is the repeated use of the same initial letter or sound of each word in a group of words. It is often used in poetry.

Examples: *Seven swans swam slowly.*
            Ducks dive directly downward into the deep.

TRY THIS

Make up your own sentences in which all (or most) of the words begin with the same letter.

The order of the alphabet from the most used letter to the least used letter would be:

e a r i o t n s
l c u d p m h
g b f y w k v x
z j q

(Concise Oxford Dictionary 11th edition 2004)

ALPHABETICAL ORDER

The English alphabet contains 26 letters. They are always written in the following order:

a b c d e f g h i j k l m n o p q r s t u v w x y z

The letters *a, e, i, o* and *u* are known as **vowels**. The letter *y* is also used as a vowel in words such as *mystery* or *cry* (short and long 'i' sound) but used as a consonant in words like *yellow* and *yard*. All the other letters are **consonants**.

To arrange words in **alphabetical order** we must look at the first letter. For example, *able* comes before *bottle* because 'a' comes before 'b'. If two or more words begin with the same letter we must look at the second letter. For example, *feel* comes before *flag* because 'e' comes before 'l'. If the first two letters are the same we must consider the third letter and so on.

TRY THIS

Write each row in alphabetical order.

| dress | drying | drill | drunk | dray |
| flush | flack | flick | flock | flimsy |

AMERICAN ENGLISH

Although people of the United States of America speak English, some of the words they use for objects differ from those we use.

Examples:

An American might turn on a *faucet* while an Australian would turn on a *tap*.

An American might like *candy* and *soda* while an Australian likes *chocolate* and *soft drink*.

American English can also differ in spelling. American spelling tends to leave out any silent or repeated letters in words.

Examples: colour – *color*   centimetre – *centimeter*
              favourite – *favorite*   cancelled – *canceled*

American films continue to bring many new words into our language.

Examples: *guy, elevator, gangster, commuter, hobo, phoney, public enemy, set-up, sucker, yes-man*

How are these words spelt in standard English?

center   theater   ax   pajamas   traveler

Find out what these American terms refer to:

diaper   schedule   sidewalk   closet   trunk
baby carriage   soda   bus boy   trash
cracker   robe   pocketbook   candy   druggist

TRY THIS

ANACHRONISMS

An anachronism is an error – deliberate or accidental – in a story or poem that places a person, event or object in the wrong historical setting.

Examples:

• Julius Caesar arriving in England in an aircraft carrier.

• A prehistoric caveman using a mobile phone.

TRY THIS

Make up your own humorous anachronisms.

ANAGRAMS

Anagrams are words made by rearranging the letters of a given word. For example, if we rearrange the letters of *war* we get *raw*. From *race* we get *care*.

Sometimes more than one word can be made, for example *meat, tame, team, mate.*

A

Make anagrams from these words:

softer, marble, melon, heart, spear, lustre, disease, battle, untied, sprite, danger

Anagrams					
ample	maple	flier	rifle	result	rustle
asleep	please	forest	softer	rinse	reins
blame	amble	garden	danger	risen	siren
bruise	rubies	general	enlarge	scalp	clasp
canoe	ocean	groan	organ	score	cores
cared	cedar	hips	ship	scream	creams
cause	sauce	horse	shore	setter	street
clean	lance	lemons	solemn	spider	prides
could	cloud	listen	tinsel	staple	pastel
dear	read	mantle	lament	swine	sinew
design	singed	marble	ramble	sword	words
disease	seaside	march	charm	table	bleat
drive	diver	north	thorn	tales	slate
earth	heart	palm	lamp	teacher	hectare
filter	trifle	please	elapse	toast	stoat
finger	fringe	priest	stripe	wolf	flow

ANALOGIES

An analogy is when we compare two things in order to highlight a similarity between them. Example: Just as a young dog is called a pup a young cat is called a kitten.

We could write this in this way: *Pup is to dog as kitten is to cat.*

TRY THIS

Add a word to complete these analogies.

geese : gaggle :   :   lion : _____
frog : tadpole :   :   whale : _____
London : England :   :   _____ : Japan
food : famine :   :   water : _____

ANECDOTES

An anecdote is a short account of an amusing or interesting event, often connected with a particular person.

Example: A famous actor sent an invitation to a famous author saying that on a certain day she would be at home. The famous author replied, 'So will I.'

ANTONYMS

Antonyms are pairs of words that have opposite meanings.

Examples: *up* and *down*; *admit* and *deny*

Write words of 5 letters that have opposite meanings to these words.

TRY THIS

lost _____   war _____   left _____

child _____   clean _____   correct _____

true _____   black _____

Antonyms

absent	*present*	familiar	*unfamiliar*	opaque	*transparent*
accept	*refuse*	famous	*unknown*	past	*future*
admit	*deny*	folly	*wisdom*	permanent	*temporary*
advance	*retreat*	forbid	*allow*	powerful	*weak*
ancient	*modern*	fresh	*stale*	punishment	*reward*
arrive	*leave*	guilty	*innocent*	present	*absent*
artificial	*genuine*	help	*hinder*	private	*public*
barren	*fertile*	hollow	*solid*	rapid	*slow*
beautiful	*ugly*	honest	*dishonest*	reap	*sow*
better	*worse*	hurry	*loiter*	reveal	*hide*
bitter	*sweet*	idle	*busy*	seldom	*often*
bless	*curse*	import	*export*	stationary	*mobile*
captivity	*freedom*	inferior	*superior*	spendthrift	*miser*
cautious	*reckless*	junior	*senior*	stubborn	*flexible*
comic	*tragic*	knowledgeable	*ignorant*	success	*failure*
compulsory	*voluntary*	liberty	*captivity*	sudden	*gradual*
conceal	*reveal*	liquid	*solid*	summer	*winter*
contract	*expand*	maximum	*minimum*	superior	*inferior*
deny	*admit*	minor	*major*	thick	*thin*
economy	*extravagance*	minority	*majority*	unique	*common*
empty	*full*	modest	*conceited*	waste	*conserve*
expensive	*cheap*	never	*always*	whole	*part*
failure	*success*	often	*seldom*	wealth	*poverty*

ARTICLES

There are three articles in English: **the**, **a** and **an**. Articles can be either definite or indefinite.

- **The** is the definite article. It is definite because it refers to a specific thing.
  Example: **The** man who lives next door is elderly.

- **A** and **an** are indefinite. Rather than referring to a specific thing, they refer to any one of a group of things.
  Example: **A** man lives next door.

- **An** is used instead of **a** in front of words that begin with a vowel (a, e, i, o, u). **An** is also used in front of words that begin with an unvoiced **h**.
  Examples: an apple, an egg, an igloo, an orange, an umbrella, an hour, but a hotel

In Functional Grammar articles are called **determiners** as they determine things about the noun. (See Functional Grammar)

ASSONANCE

Assonance is the repetition of a vowel sound. It differs from a standard rhyme as the whole words do not necessarily rhyme and it does not need to be at the end of a line of poetry, but can be found throughout a line of a poem or a sentence in a story.

Examples: If you use your br**ai**n and travel by tr**ai**n, it saves you a lot of p**ai**n.

The s**o**ggy, sp**o**tty d**o**g w**a**ndered **o**ff.

AUSTRALIAN ENGLISH

There are many words and phrases that are peculiar to Australia. These words have developed through such things as discoveries, inventions, sports and pastimes. These special Australian words and phrases are common and colourful in our every day language, but are difficult for non-Australians to understand.

A visitor from overseas would probably be perplexed if you said *'Charlie's a bonzer bloke, but a bit of a bludger. He likes his tucker and skites to the sheilas'.*

Find out what these words and phrases refer to.

galah, goanna, chuck a u-ey, damper, drongo, lagerphone, whinger, wowser, yabby, mulga, paddock, kelpie, joey, jackeroo, g'day, bloke, dunny

TRY THIS

AUTOBIOGRAPHY

An autobiography is the story of a person's life written by the person.

AUXILIARY VERBS

Auxiliary verbs are sometimes called 'helper' verbs. They are used with other verbs or participles to make a complete verb. Some common auxiliary verbs include:

am   are   is   we   were   be   being   has   have   had   shall   will   might   may   must   could   should   would

Auxiliary verbs provide us with a clearer sense of time – present, past, future – as well as illustrating obligation and possibility.

Present	*I **am jumping** the fence. Sally **is playing** hockey.*
Past	*They **have completed** the work.* *She **had seen** the accident.*
Future	*Mike **will come** later. I **shall be** cheering for you.*
Ability	*I **can kick** the ball into the goal.* *All of us **could hear** the spooky noise.*
Possibility	*Tom **might come** too.* *Joanne **may stay** at my place.*
Obligation	*She **should be** eating less junk food.* *You **must stop** right now.*

Auxiliary verbs along with non-finite verbs (infinitives or participles) form compound verbs (ie verbs made up of more than one word). They are also known as verb phrases.
(See also Participles; Verbs)

The word hijinks has three consecutive dotted letters. Can you think of an island of the Pacific (not far from Australia) that also has three dotted letters in a row?

B

BIAS

Bias is often found in persuasive writing and informative writing, such as reviews, biographies and news articles.

Bias is the preference for or dislike of one thing over another. It does not need to have a logical explanation. It is the opinion of the author.

Example: *Bozo Coffee is tastier and healthier than all the others.*

The words **facetious** and **abstemious** both contain all the vowels in the order they come in the alphabet. Do you know what each word means?

BIBLIOGRAPHY

A bibliography enables you to find information about a particular topic.

A bibliography is an alphabetical list of books and other reference material that a writer has used to obtain information when producing their own work.

A bibliography can also be a list of everything written by a particular writer or about a particular subject.

Example: a *Bibliography of Australian Wildlife.*

BIOGRAPHY

A biography is the story of someone's life written by another person. Many famous people have had their lives recorded by another person. This is one way historical events and lives can be preserved for future generations.

CASE

Case reflects the relationship between a noun or pronoun and a verb. In English there are three main cases:

- subjective (or nominative)
- objective (or accusative)
- possessive (or genitive).

These are determined by the position of the noun or pronoun in the sentence.

Subjective and objective case

Look at the following sentence. *Bruno hit the ball.*

The **subject** of the sentence is *Bruno*. He is the person doing the hitting (performing the action). The **object** of the sentence is the *ball* – it is the thing being hit (receiving the action).

Bruno is in **the subjective case** and the *ball* is in the **objective case**.

- Nouns and most pronouns do not change their form regardless of whether they are in the subjective case or objective case:
  Bruno hit the ball.   The ball hit Bruno.
- Some pronouns vary in form:

Subject	Object
She He We	her him us
They I	them me

Possessive case

The possessive case refers to ownership:

Davina's ball   the owner's ball   my ball

(See Apostrophes – Possession p.76)

Upper and lower case

Case also refers to the difference between capital and non-capital letters in writing.

- Upper case = capital letters, used for proper nouns and at the beginning of sentences.
- Lower case = regular small letters of the alphabet

BLAKE'S ENGLISH GUIDE

CLASSIFYING WORDS

Most objects can be classified into a group. For example, *sparrows, hawks, owls* and *wrens* all belong to the group called **birds**.

Words can be classified into parts of speech. For example *dog, cat, table* and *chair* are all **nouns**, while *run, hop, skip* and *chase* are all **verbs**.

Sorting words into specific groups or classifications of sounds, patterns, meanings etc is a powerful tool for improving spelling. For example, 'ai' sounding words: stain, again, brain, main etc.

The word queue begins with a consonant followed by four vowels. The first letter q also says the name of the word.

CLAUSES

A clause is a group of words containing a verb. Clauses differ from phrases in that they have both a subject (telling part) and verb (doing part). A sentence consists of one or more clauses.

Examples:

*She **accepted** the gift.*

This sentence has **one** verb and therefore one clause.

*She **accepted** the gift when she **won** the race.*

This sentence has **two** verbs. It therefore has two clauses.

There are two main types of clauses:

The **principal clause** (or main clause) is the backbone of the sentence. It can often make a simple sentence on its own. Example: *The children went home.*

A **subordinate clause** (or dependent clause) can act as an adjective, adverb or noun and depends upon the principal clause for its meaning. Example: *before the sun went down* as in *The children went home before the sun went down.*

CLICHÉ

A cliché is a saying or idea which has lost its freshness or power through overuse.

Examples: *slow as a snail   hard as a rock*

mad as a hatter   pretty as a picture

Many clichés are roundabout ways of saying something simpler and often only confuse the reader.

Examples: *on account of the fact that*   (use *because*)

                         is of the opinion that   (use *thinks*)

However some clichés may be exactly what you are trying to say and do not need to be avoided.

Examples: *last but not least; lost for words*

Make up your own expressions for the following:

slow as _____   hard as _____

mad as _____   pretty as _____

TRY THIS

CLOZE

Cloze is a reading activity to test comprehension, in which a passage of writing has a number of words removed with blank spaces in their place. The reader must predict what the missing word is. Different words may be used that still retain the correct meaning. To make a successful cloze activity, no word should be removed in the first sentence of a passage and then only one word in twelve or so after.

Find a passage of writing that interests you. Using a computer, type out the passage, deleting a number of important words and inserting a short blank line in their place. Print it out and challenge others to fill in the missing words.

Example: *I have seen many bushfires but never such a one as this. The _____ was blowing like a hurricane and the _____ leapt above the trees. I became very _____.*

TRY THIS

COLLOCATION (TWIN WORDS)

The practice of using two words which commonly go together, always in the same order, and have a well-known meaning is called collocation.

COLLOCATION continued

Examples:

alive and kicking	hammer and tongs	rough and tumble
bacon and eggs	hard and fast	round and round
beck and call	head and shoulders	safe and sound
body and soul	heart and soul	salt and pepper
bread and butter	heaven and earth	short and sweet
broad daylight	here and there	sixes and sevens
cats and dogs	hide and seek	slowly and surely
crystal clear	high and dry	spick and span
down and out	high and low	stuff and nonsense
excruciating pain	length and breadth	sunshine and
facts and figures	lock and key	shadow
fair and square	long and short	tall and thin
fame and fortune	neck and neck	there and then
far and wide	off and on	thick and thin
far away	one and all	time and tide
fast and furious	out and about	tooth and nail
fire and water	over and above	tried and true
first and foremost	over and done with	up and going
fits and starts	over and over	ups and downs
flesh and blood	part and parcel	watch and wait
forgive and forget	peace and plenty	ways and means
free and easy	rack and ruin	
fully aware	rank and file	
give and take	root and branch	
hale and hearty	rough and ready	

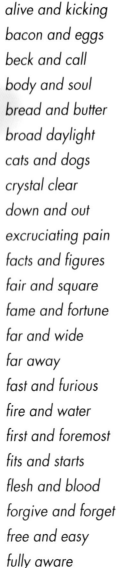

COLLOQUIALISMS

People often use certain types of well-known expressions
to make their speech more interesting or their writing more
realistic. For example, instead of saying 'she fell off the horse'
you might say 'she came a cropper'. Instead of saying 'I am
going to have a quick sleep' you might say 'I'm going to have
forty winks'.

a) Make up some humorous colloquialisms to describe a person who is:

sleepy   stupid   snobbish   exhausted

attentive   lying

b) Match the colloquial expressions on the left with their meanings:

a bit steep   to be tossed out or fired

a smack in the eye   far too expensive

to take it lying down   to come to an end

to peter out   to his maximum capacity

to take the rap   very discouraging, an insult

to get the boot   to take the blame for
                                      someone else

for all he was worth   not to offer any resistance

COMPARATIVE AND SUPERLATIVE

Many adjectives and adverbs allow for degrees of comparison between two or more people or items. There are three degrees of comparison:

- positive – used to describe a single thing
- comparative – used to compare two things
- superlative – used to compare three or more things.

In most cases **er** is added to the end of a word to show *comparative degree* and **est** is added to the end of a word to show *superlative degree*.

The first public library in Australia to be funded by the government was the Public Library in Melbourne founded in 1853.

Positive	Comparative	Superlative
brave	braver	bravest
big	bigger	biggest
fair	fairer	fairest
noisy	noisier	noisiest
beautiful	more beautiful	most beautiful
bad	worse	worst
good	better	best

BLAKE'S ENGLISH GUIDE

COMPOUND WORDS

Compound words are two or more words joined together to make one new word.

Some compound words are hyphenated but often with common use over time, when the word becomes accepted it drops the hyphen.

Almost any combination of parts of speech is possible.

noun + noun – *hailstorm*	adjective + noun – *blackbird*
noun + adjective – *headstrong*	adjective + adjective – *blue-green*
pronoun + noun – *she-oak*	adjective + verb – *highlight*
verb + noun – *spitfire*	verb + adverb – *farewell*
adverb + verb – *outgoing*	adverb + noun – *onlooker*
adverb + preposition – *therein*	preposition + noun – *underworld*

TRY THIS

Make up your own crazy compound words for foods, animals, sports or machines.

Examples:

two nouns – *wallabyfish* is a fish that looks like a wallaby.

two verbs – *danceboxing* is dance moves and boxing combined.

adjective and noun – *hoverbike* is a bicycle that hovers above the ground.

Compound Words

The word there contains its opposite here.

barefoot	hailstorm	rainbow
blackbird	hamburger	roadworks
coastline	handcuff	seahorse
commonplace	handkerchief	sheepskin
countryside	hayfever	shipwreck
courtyard	headlight	signwriter
cutthroat	headstrong	skateboard
downstairs	heartbreak	spoilsport
downstream	horseback	sunglasses
dragnet	houseboat	tombstone
driftwood	inside	toothache
earthquake	lookout	walkover
elsewhere	outboard	waterfall
farewell	pineapple	

COMPREHENSION

The dictionary defines comprehension as the 'act or power of understanding'. Comprehension is a cognitive process requiring such skills as observing, conceptualising, re-organising, evaluating, inferring, appreciating, reconstructing and sharing.

Comprehension involves analytical thinking processes that go far beyond merely understanding the concepts represented by individual words and sentences. It requires and demands a process of analysis, judgment and evaluation.

There are three levels of comprehension:

1 Literal Comprehension
- recognising sentence meaning
- recognising and recalling details
- recognising main ideas
- recognising and recalling sequence

2 Inferential/Interpretative Comprehension
- inferring main ideas
- inferring supporting details
- predicting outcomes
- relating cause and effect
- inferring character
- distinguishing between fact and opinion
- distinguishing between reality and fantasy

3 Critical/Evaluative Comprehension
- examining information, ideas and opinions for meaning, values, emotion, effectiveness and design
- recognising points of view
- detecting bias, stereotyping, author's stance and motives
- identifying cultural beliefs
- articulating own ideas, views and understanding
- understanding how texts can manipulate emotions, reinforce values and undermine beliefs
- identifying voices – silent, absent, marginalised

CONCLUSIONS

After we have been given relevant information we can usually make a logical conclusion. Drawing conclusions is part of inferential comprehension.

Example: *All birds lay eggs. A magpie is a bird.*

The first sentence tells us something about birds: they all lay eggs. Now we can correctly conclude a magpie would also lay eggs.

We can always draw logical conclusions from a sentence providing the information we are given is based on fact and not on opinion.

Example:

Joe James is sixty years old. He has never seen the ocean.

Here are some things you could conclude about Joe James:

(a) Joe James is a male.

(b) Joe James is over fifty years old.

(c) Joe James is blind.

Conclusions (a) and (b) are based on the facts given in the statement. However, the statement does not support the conclusion (c) that Joe is blind (it only infers it). There may be other reasons why Joe James has never seen the ocean. He may have lived in central Australia all his life.

TRY THIS

Make up some statements of your own and get others to determine the conclusions based on fact.

CONCORD

Concord means agreement. In English grammar concord means agreement between a subject and its verb which both must have the same number, so if a subject is singular the verb must be **singular**.

Examples: *He **is** here. Sam **likes** ice-cream.*

And if the subject is plural the verb must also be plural.

Examples: *They **are** here. We **like** ice-cream.*

When a subject consists of two singular nouns joined by and we must use a plural verb. Example: *Jack and Jill are here.*

However:

- If the two subjects are joined by **or** or **nor** the singular verb is used. Example: *Neither Jack nor Jill **is** here.*
- If two **plural** subjects are joined by **or** or **nor** we use the **plural** verb. Example: *The boys **or** girls **are** coming.*
- Words that refer to sums or quantities such as length, money amounts and so on take singular verbs.
  Examples: *Fifty kilometres **is** a long way. Ten dollars **is** all I've got.*
- Collective nouns like *herd, bunch, flock* etc usually take a singular verb. Examples: *The flock of ducks is in the garden. The bunch of grapes was on the table.*

However, this rule sometimes varies. Example: *The senate is to meet today.* Here the singular is used because the senate is **one** body. Now consider this: *The senate are unable to agree.* Because it is a number of people who make up the senate who are unable to agree then we use the **plural** verb *are.*

This table shows the number of the verb we must use with pronouns.

Pronoun	he she it	I	we you they
	is	am	are
	was	was	were
	does	do	do
	has	have	have

CONJUNCTIONS

Conjunctions are words that are used to join words or groups of words.

Examples: *Peter **and** John rode their bikes.*

   We did not come. We were ill. becomes:
   *We did not come **because** we were ill.*

There are different types of conjunctions.

Coordinating conjunctions join parts of a sentence that are of a similar type and of equal importance.

Examples: *I like fish **and** chips.* (nouns linked)

*The dog ran across the yard **and** into its kennel.* (two adverbial phrases linked)

*My team played well **but** we were beaten.* (two main clauses joined)

The most common coordinating conjunctions are:
and but for nor or so yet

Subordinating conjunctions are used to join a subordinate clause to the rest of the sentence.

Example: *We lost the match **because** we played badly.*

Some common subordinating conjunctions are:

after	*so long as*	*when*
although	*that*	*whenever*
as	*then*	*where*
because	*therefore*	*whereas*
before	*though*	*wherever*
once	*unless*	*whether*
since	*until*	*while*

Correlative conjunctions are used in pairs.

Examples: *You can have **either** eggs **or** bacon for breakfast.*

*She is **neither** tall **nor** short.*

*Her brother is **both** handsome **and** intelligent.*

Some common correlative conjunctions are:

as… as	*both…and*	*not only… but also*
either…or	*neither…nor*	*not…but whether…or*

Conjunctions usually occur between the things they are joining, but this is not always so. A sentence can begin with a conjunction.

Example: ***While** in Sydney, I visited the Opera House.*

In the past it was frowned upon to begin a sentence with *and* or *but*. Today it is acceptable to do so when you have good reason, such as for a particular effect.

Example: *He found his keys. He found his car. He found his wallet.*
***And** he found happiness again.*

CONSONANTS

Consonants are letters of the alphabet used as symbols to represent speech sounds. To make the sounds of consonants, the air is in some way impeded as the sound is spoken.

- Consonant sounds made with a small explosion in letters such as 'p' in *park*, 'b' in *bark*, 't' in *tap*, 'd' in *dip*, 'k' in *kill* and 'g' in *got* are called **plosives**.

- Consonant sounds made by air passing through the nose in letters such as 'm' in *mat*, 'n' in *nag* are called **nasals**.

- Consonant sounds made by friction of the air as in such letters as 'f' in *file*, 'v' in *vile*, 'r' in *ran* and 's' in *sat* are called **fricatives**.

- Consonant sounds made by a combination of explosion and friction, such as 'ch' in *chill* and 'j' in *jam*, are called **affricates**.

- In the consonant sound 'l' as in *lack*, the air passes around the tongue so 'l' is called a **lateral**.

- The consonant sounds 'w' as in *way* or *won* and 'y' as in *yes* or *year* are called **semi vowels** because the obstruction of the passage of air is extremely slight.

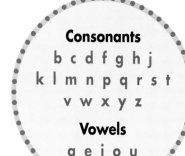

Consonants
b c d f g h j
k l m n p q r s t
v w x y z

Vowels
a e i o u

CONTRACTIONS

In writing and speech we often combine two words to form one word. In doing so, we usually replace a letter, or letters, with an apostrophe. These shortened words are called **contractions**.

The following is a list of contractions in common use, classified according to their combining words.

NOT	*isn't wasn't doesn't can't won't don't mustn't aren't didn't weren't wouldn't shouldn't haven't couldn't hasn't*
HAVE	*I've you've we've they've could've should've would've*
WILL	*I'll you'll he'll she'll they'll there'll it'll*
IS / HAS	*he's she's it's who's there's that's where's what's*
WOULD / HAD	*I'd you'd he'd she'd we'd they'd*
ARE	*we're you're they're*
AM	*I'm*

DEFINITIONS

When we define a term we do two things. First, we place the term in a certain class, and second, we indicate how it differs from other items in that class.

Here are some definitions:

pennon **a long, narrow flag**, triangular or swallow-tailed.

jabiru **Australia's only stork**, white with glossy green-black head, neck and tail.

The highlighted part of each definition places the object in its class, while the rest distinguishes it from other objects in that same class.

Suggestions for making definitions

- The classification should be as specific as possible. To define a jabiru as just a bird would be too general.
- The object you are defining must be easily distinguished from other objects in that class. To say a car is a four-wheeled vehicle still leaves trucks and taxis in that class.
- A definition should be as simple as possible. Not too many people would understand that milk is an oleaginous derivative of mammals.
- The object of definition and the definition offered should have the same grammatical structure. Decapitation is not when they cut off a person's head, it is the act of cutting off a person's head.
- A definition should not use the word being defined, or one formed from it.

*Australia's first book arcade was opened by E.W. Cole in Melbourne in 1873.
In 1883, Cole opened a bigger and better book arcade. By 1900, it was considered to be the world's largest bookshop.*

DEWEY DECIMAL SYSTEM

Melvil Dewey (1851–1931), an American librarian, devised a system for classifying library books. His system is still used by many schools and public libraries today.

His classifications divide non-fiction books into ten broad categories.

000– 99 General works (encyclopedias and similar works)
100–199 Philosophy (how people think and what they believe)
200–299 Religion (including mythology and religions of the world)

300–399 Social sciences (folklore and legends, government, manners and customs, vocations)
400–499 Language (dictionaries, grammar)
500–599 Pure science (mathematics, astronomy, chemistry, botany)
600–699 Technology (applied sciences – aviation, building, engineering, homemaking)
700–799 Arts (photography, drawing, painting, music, sports)
800–899 Literature (plays, poetry)
900–999 History (ancient and modern, geography, travel)

Each of these sections is further divided numerically and alphabetically for accuracy in classification.
Example: 786.10924 CHO – *Chopin: A Biography*

DICTIONARY

A dictionary contains words listed in alphabetical order along with their pronunciation, meanings and usage. Most dictionaries also list the part of speech of each word, often abbreviated, eg *noun (n)*, *verb (v)*, *adjective (adj)* etc.

Example: gaggle *n.* a flock of geese.

After each definition the dictionary usually lists the etymology (origin) of the word. This is often shown in square brackets.

Examples: [L] = Latin   [OE] = Old English   [F] = French

DIALOGUE

When writing stories or plays, your characters will talk to each other, or sometimes even talk to themselves. In stories this is referred to as direct speech. *(See Direct Speech)* The words actually spoken are indicated by placing speech marks (or inverted commas) at the beginning and end of what is said. In plays and TV or movie scripts it is called dialogue. No speech marks are used, instead each character's speech begin on a new line, following their name and any stage directions.

Example:

WOLF: Little pig, little pig, let me in.
PIG: *(nervously)* Not by the hair on my chinny-chin-chin.
WOLF: *(loudly)* Then I'll huff and I'll puff and I'll blow your house in.

Through the words they use and how their speech is described, the audience can learn a lot about the type of character they are.

D

DIGRAPHS

Digraphs are pairs of letters that represent a single speech sound.

Examples: **ea** in *meat, treat* **ch** in *chips, chocolate*

ai in *train, brain* **sh** in *shop, bush*

oo in *foot, soot* **ng** in *ring, song*

DIPHTHONGS

Diphthong is a speech sound consisting of a glide from one vowel to another within one syllable.

Examples: **ei** in *vein* **ou** in *loud*

DIRECT SPEECH

Speech can be reported directly or indirectly.

Direct speech, or dialogue, is the exact words spoken by a person in a piece of text. It is usually enclosed in quotation marks, also called inverted commas. Single marks ('… ') or double ones ("…") can be used.

Example: *'I am writing a story,' said Meg.*

Quotation marks are placed before the first word spoken and after the last word spoken. A comma or any other punctuation, such as a question mark or an exclamation mark, is always included within the quotation marks.

Examples: *"What's your story about?" asked Alex.*

'I won first prize!' Jess exclaimed.

Now look at this sentence.

Kristy said, 'Look at that fluffy cat.'

Here the unspoken words come first. Notice that the first word spoken begins with a capital letter.

The unspoken words can also come in the middle of the sentence, between the spoken words. This is sometimes called a broken quotation.

Example: *'The problem with cats,' said Mike, 'is that they make me sneeze.'*

Notice two pairs of quotation marks are used. The second half of the spoken sentence does not need a capital letter.

EPILOGUE

An epilogue is a short addition or concluding section at the end of a literary work, often dealing with the future of the characters who were introduced in the story.

EPITAPHS

Epitaphs are the words we see inscribed on a grave or tomb. Some examples of rather odd epitaphs include:

I'm sick and tired of being sick and tired.
Here lies Les Moore. No more, no less.

I TOLD YOU I WAS ILL

EPITHET

An epithet is a term used to characterise a person or thing.

Examples: *blood-red sky*   *Alexander the Great*

It can also be a term used as a descriptive substitute for the name of a person.

Examples: Elvis Presley – *The King*   Dwayne Johnson – *The Rock*

Sometimes epithets are derogatory, drawing attention to a person's particular appearance or personality.

Examples: *egghead* – an intellectual
                      four-eyes – someone who wears glasses

EPONYMS

An eponym is a word that originated from the name of someone.
Examples:

- *Braille* – after Louis Braille, a Frenchman, who developed a way for sight impaired people to read through a system of raised dots.

- *Morse code* – after the American, Samuel Morse, who invented this system of communication.

- *Lamington* – this famous Australian cake was first served to Lord Lamington, Governor of Queensland from 1896 to 1901, and named in his honour.

- *Pasteurisation* – a method of food preservation invented by and named for French chemist, Louis Pasteur.

ETYMOLOGY

Etymology is the derivation and formation of a word. Every word we use has a history or a story of how it was born.

In a dictionary a word's etymology is given, enclosed in square brackets.

The etymology of some common words:

- *lettuce* [from a Latin word meaning 'milk-giving plant']
- *mushroom* [from a French word meaning 'moss']
- *volcano* [from the Roman god of fire, *Vulcan*]
- *leopard* [from Greek word *leopardos* meaning 'lion-tiger']
- *poodle* [from German word *pudelhund* meaning 'splash dog']

Modern English includes countless words borrowed from other languages, although Old English has always remained at the core of the English language.

Early examples of words from outside of England came with the arrival of Christianity in Britain in 597 CE. A number of Latin words of a religious character, for which no Old English words existed, were added to the English language.

Examples include *Christian, mass, priest, candle, altar, bishop.*

Towards the end of the eighth century the Danish Vikings began invading Britain and many settled among the inhabitants. Words taken from Danish include *call, clumsy, fellow, hit, knife, husband, they, them, want.*

In 1066, when William of Normandy invaded and began nearly 300 years of Norman rule, French words such as *comedy, charity, humour, justice, tragedy, trespass* were integrated into English. In fact, English borrowed so many French words, today we often have two words for the same thing (synonyms). Examples: *wed* (OE) / *marry* (F); *child* (OE) / *infant* (F). Old English words were usually simpler. For example, the word *conflagration* might sound impressive in a novel but if your house was on fire and you needed help fast, it is much easier to yell 'Fire! Fire!'.

During the Renaissance in Europe (14th–17th century), we borrowed lots of words from Latin and Greek. These include *computer, accommodate, master, radius, senior.* From Greek came *cinema, telegraph, telephone, uranium.*

By 1650 the language, with all its foreign influences, was known

One of Australia's most famous authors and poets, Henry Lawson, was deaf from the age of 14.

as Modern English. However, the language is constantly evolving and continues to add words.

Examples:

Technical Terms:	*bacteria, electron, oxygen, supersonic*
American Words:	*commuter, elevator, gangster, racket*
World Wars:	*paratroops, Gestapo, blitz, U-boat, bulldozer*
Italian:	*spaghetti, pizza, graffiti*
Russian:	*vodka, rouble*
Indian:	*turban, curry*
Japanese:	*karaoke, sushi*

These borrowings have taken place because of migrations from these countries into English-speaking countries or English speakers living overseas. Today English can truly be said to be an international language.

EUPHEMISM

A euphemism is a mild or vague word or phrase used in place of another, to disguise an unpleasant fact or to replace an unacceptably blunt or offensive expression. For example, we may prefer to say that someone has 'passed away', rather than to say they have 'died'. Some euphemisms are useful while others make our speaking and writing vague and complicated.

Some examples of euphemisms used today are:

Euphemism	**Meaning**
to put an animal down / put it to sleep	*to kill an animal*
to go to the bathroom / powder one's nose	*to go to the toilet*
in the family way / has a bun in the oven	*pregnant*

FABLES

A fable is a short story, often about animals with human characteristics, that teaches a lesson or moral about how to behave. Probably the best known fables are those written by *Aesop* (5th Century BCE), including *The Hare and the Tortoise* and *The Fox and the Grapes*.

FACT AND OPINION

Facts are statements that can be proved. Opinions are personal feelings or ideas about something or someone else.

To decide whether something is a fact or opinion consider the following:

- Can the statement be proved? If so, it is a fact, eg *Europe is a continent.*
- Do others agree with the statement? Many people may agree with an opinion, but that does not make it a fact, eg *Dogs are the cleverest of all animals.*

FAIRYTALES

Fairytales are imaginary narratives traditionally set in an indistinct time 'Long, long ago', with characters such as princes and princesses, kings and queens, witches and fairies, and talking animals. Usually an element of magic is involved.

They were written to entertain young children, but they can also teach children about values and behaviour, as many fairytales have a moral or message at the end.

FIGURATIVE LANGUAGE

Figurative language is the use of words that do not hold their literal meaning.

Examples: My little brother *drives me up the wall.*
             (makes me very annoyed)

             Our teacher told us to *pull our socks up.*
             (try harder)

Commonly used phrases are often referred to as 'a figure of speech'. *(See also Idioms; Imagery; Metaphors; Similes)*

FOLKTALES

Almost any traditional narrative, either oral or literary, from any part of the world can come under the heading of folktale. Its diverse forms include myths and legends, fairytales and fables.

FOREIGN WORDS AND PHRASES

The English language has adopted a number of foreign words and phrases, particularly in our legal system.

The following have come from (L) Latin, (G) German, (Gr) Greek, (F) French.

Word	Origin	Meaning
ad hoc	(L)	for this special purpose: impromptu
ad infinitum	(L)	for ever; to infinity
ad nauseum	(L)	to the point of disgust
à la carte	(F)	from the full menu
alter ego	(L)	one's other self
auf wiedersehen	(G)	till we meet again
au naturel	(F)	in a natural state
au revoir	(F)	till we meet again
bona fide	(L)	in good faith; genuine
bon voyage	(F)	have a good journey
carpe diem	(L)	enjoy today
carte blanche	(F)	full powers
caveat emptor	(L)	let the buyer beware
compos mentis	(L)	of sound mind; sane
de facto	(L)	in fact
double entendre	(F)	double meaning
esprit de corps	(F)	group spirit
fait accompli	(F)	an accomplished fact
hoi polloi	(Gr)	the common people
hors d'oeuvre	(F)	appetiser served before main meal
in loco parentis	(L)	in the place of a parent
in memoriam	(L)	in memory (of)
ipso facto	(L)	obvious from the facts

FUNCTIONAL GRAMMAR

Refer to the chart in the *Grammar* entry for functional grammar terms and their uses. For more detailed information about Functional Grammar see Del Merrick's excellent book *Blake's Grammar Guide*.

GENDER

Look at this sentence:

My mother and father gave the poor dog a bone.

Mother is the name of a female person (she).

Father is the name of a male person (he).

Dog can be either male or female (it).

Bone is neither male nor female – it has no gender (it).

- Words which refer to 'female' are said to belong to the feminine gender.

  Examples: *daughter   queen   aunt   waitress*

- Words which refer to 'male' are said to belong to the masculine gender.

  Examples: *son   king   uncle   waiter*

- Words which refer to either male or female belong to the common gender.

  Examples: *teacher   cousin   friend*

- Words which are neither the male nor female belong to the neuter gender.

  Examples: *desk   book   apple*

Some words have a masculine and feminine form, such as *prince, princess; host, hostess*. In modern English, many of these distinctions have been dropped, for example the words *actor* and *hero* can refer to a male or a female.

GENERALISATIONS

We can use facts about people or things to draw conclusions. Read these sentences:

Michelle and Sam like apricots. Mr and Mrs Smith like apricots.

Susan hates apricots. Jack and Tameika like apricots and peaches.

From the facts above you could draw a **general conclusion** that some people like apricots. A general conclusion arrived at in this way is called a generalisation. Generalisations may be based on lots of facts or only a few.

GENRE

One feature that helps us to determine the differences among texts is the purpose for which a piece is written. The entire structure of the text is determined by the purpose. When we study the way a text is structured to achieve a specific purpose we are studying its genre.

For example if a piece of writing is a narrative it will be different from the structure of an exposition. In other words it will be written in a different genre.

	TEXT TYPES	GENRE
A. IMAGINATIVE	Poetry	rhymes, jingles, couplets, limericks, cinquain, haiku, free verse songs
	Narrative	myths and legends, fairy tales, science fiction, historical, fiction, fables
	Drama	play scripts, improvisation, movies, mime
B. INFORMATIVE	Recount	diary, letter, e-mail, autobiography, factual recount, journal, literary recount
	Procedure	instructions, recipes, experiments, directions
	Report	documentary, biography, scientific report, current affairs, news, field work
	Explanation	mechanical, magazine, life cycle, medical journal
C. PERSUASIVE	Exposition	review, advertising, editorial, documentary
	Discussion	debate, panel talks, documents, current affairs

GOBBLEDEGOOK

Gobbledegook is language or text that uses too many words and excessive jargon so it becomes convoluted and difficult to understand. This occurs when people try to sound clever by using too many complex words to describe something simple. When a euphemism goes too far it can become gobbledegook, for example, referring to a ballpoint pen as a 'manual ink processor', or calling a shovel a 'manual labour emplacement evacuator'.

This kind of language is used increasingly in business with words like 'pro-active', 'downsizing' and 'vertically integrated' commonly heard.

GRAMMAR (QUICK REFERENCE)

Traditional and Functional Terms

Traditional Grammar focuses on the structure of sentences and texts we create.
Functional Grammar takes into account what we talk about, to whom we are talking and how we will exchange the message.

TRADITIONAL	FUNCTIONAL	MEANING
Articles Definite: the; Indefinite: a, an	Determiners	Determine things about the noun eg *the* bike, *a* job, *an* elephant
Adjective (and adjectival phrase) (Describing Words)	Attribute	Adds meaning to or describes a noun or noun group
Adverb (and adverbial phrase)	Circumstance	Adds meaning to a verb, adjective or other adverb. Tells *how, when, why, where* about the verb (process).
Auxiliary Verb (Modifiers) Helping (verbs)	Auxiliary Verb	Words that are used in front of the verb to show future tense. (I *will* help you) or in front of present and past participles. (We *had* left the room. They *are* sitting down. He *has* found her.)
Clause	Clause	A group of words with a finite verb. (A verb that has a subject.)
Connections between different words, sentences and paragraphs (Cohesion)	Cohesion Conjunction Ellipsis / Substitution Pronoun Reference Lexical Chain Repetition Theme / Rheme (Related Words)	The linking of ideas in a text.
Conjunction (Joining Words)	Conjunction	A joining word in a text. Joins words, phrases or clauses.
Inflection	Inflection	A suffix added to a noun or verb to show number or tense. (*The boys are playing football.*)
Main Idea at beginning of a clause	Theme and Rheme	The main idea (theme) is placed at the beginning of a clause for emphasis. The rheme is the remaining words in the clause.
Mood *Imperative* *Declarative* *Interrogative*	Mood	The verb form which indicates statements, commands or questions.
Mood Subjunctive	Modality This shows how certain we are of things.	Wishes, certainty, doubts, hopes, probability, expressed through modals, eg *might, should, must, quite, rather, definitely.*
Noun (Naming Word) (and noun groups or pronouns)	Participants	The people, animals or things involved in the events of the text.

TRADITIONAL	FUNCTIONAL	MEANING
Participle *Present participle* *Past participle*	Participle	Part of a verb in a verb group or used as a verbal adjective. Present: *She **is** running to school.* Past: *She **has** run to school.*
Phrase	Phrase	A group of words with no subject or finite verb. Phrases do the work of a noun, adverb or adjective. They add detail to sentences.
Preposition	Preposition	Relates a noun in time or space to the rest of the sentence. Introduces a prepositional phrase, eg *up, in, under, like*.
Principal (Main) Clause	Main Clause	A clause that makes sense by itself. It can stand on its own.
Pronoun	Pronoun	A word that stands in place of a noun, eg the girl – *she*, the boys – *they*.
Sentence	Clause Complex	One or more clauses linked together in meaning. One must be the main clause. Begins with a capital letter and ends with a full stop, question mark or exclamation mark.
Subject and Predicate	Agent (Participant) and (Action Process)	The subject is the subject of the verb. The predicate contains the finite verb and modifiers. *The boy* (subject) *kicked the ball over the fence* (predicate).
Subordinate (Dependent Clause)	Dependent Clause Embedded Clause	A clause supporting a main clause. A dependent clause cannot stand alone. *We walked* (main) *where the grass was cut* (dependent).
Tense Tells us when something is occurring – Present, Past, Future	Tense Present, Past, Future	The form of the verb that indicates when an action is taking place. Present: *The boy is walking.* Past: *The boy walked.* Future: *The boy will walk.*
Verb (Doing Word)	Process	A part of speech (or word) which states the action of what is happening or has happened. These are 'doing', 'saying', 'thinking', 'feeling', 'being' and 'having' processes.
Voice *Active* *Passive*	Voice *Active* *Passive*	In the active voice the subject is the doer. *The girl bit the lolly.* In the passive voice the subject is acted upon. *The lolly was bitten by the girl.* In Functional Grammar the doer is the theme in the active voice and the receiver of the action in the passive voice and is in the theme position.

HISTORY OF ENGLISH

The following is a brief description of how the English language developed and is still developing.

English is a living language. Some words become obsolete and drop out of use (eg *dearworth, thee, thou*), while new words keep it growing and evolving.

The history of the English language really begins in the fifth century, when three Germanic tribes – the Angles, the Saxons and the Jutes – invaded Britain, which was then under the rule of a declining Roman Empire. The land became known as *Angle Land* (England) and the language was called *Anglo-Saxon*. This is the language we now call *Old English*. Between the years 450 and 1066 CE Old English was spoken by most of the inhabitants of England. Old English gave us many simple words we still use today like *father, mother, brother, sister* and *love*. However in the ninth century the Angles, Saxons and Jutes were conquered by the Vikings from Denmark and Norway, and Old English borrowed many words from these Scandinavians, such as *freckle, skull, walrus* (meaning 'whale horse').

In 1066 CE, William the Conqueror, from Normandy (now France), invaded and conquered England. The Normans became the landowners, speaking French, while the Angles and Saxons became slaves, speaking Old English. Saxon servants waiting on French noblemen began incorporating certain French words into their vocabulary. For example instead of sheep they had to serve *mouton* (mutton); rather than cattle their meat was called by the French word *boeuf* (beef). In time, this French influence created a newer language called *Middle English*.

The language we speak today is known as *Modern English*. Today our language is constantly evolving as new words from foreign countries, inventions and technology enter into everyday use.

The word **uncopyrightable** is the longest word that can be written without repeating a letter of the alphabet.

HOMONYMS

A homonym is a word that has the same pronunciation or spelling as another word but a different meaning.

There are two types of homonyms: homographs and homophones.

Homographs

Homographs are words that are spelt the same but have a different meaning.

Examples: *Sally has **fair** hair.*

*We had lots of fun at the **fair**.*

*When you play sport you should always be **fair**.*

Although homographs are spelt the same, they may not always have the same pronunciation. Thus, *bow* meaning a weapon as in 'bow and arrows', and *bow* meaning to bend at the waist, are homographs but are not pronounced the same.

Word	Meanings	
bank	sloping ground (noun)	place where money is kept (noun)
bark	covering of a tree (noun)	cry of a dog (noun)
bass	fish (noun)	low (usually of a voice) (adjective)
bear	animal (noun)	to carry (verb)
conduct	behaviour (noun)	direct an orchestra (verb)
content	book contents (noun)	happy (adjective)
converse	opposite (noun)	talk with someone (verb)
convict	prisoner (noun)	to prove guilty of an offence (verb)
desert	dry sandy area (noun)	to abandon (verb)
fair	market (noun)	blonde (adjective)
lead	a soft metal (noun)	to show the way (verb)
leaves	plural of leaf (noun)	departs (verb)
minute	unit of time (noun)	very small (adjective)
object	thing (noun)	to express disapproval (verb)
present	gift (noun)	to give to (verb)
refuse	rubbish (noun)	to decline (verb)
sow	female pig (noun)	to scatter seed (verb)
tear	fluid secreted by the eye (noun)	to rip up (verb)
wind	moving air currents (noun)	to coil around something (verb)

Homophones

Homophones are words that are pronounced the same but have different meanings and may have different spellings.

Examples:

sea / see   guessed / guest   medal / meddle

aisle – isle – I'll	metal – mettle
air – heir	minor – miner
birth – berth	moose – mousse
bail – bale	more – moor – maw
bald – bawled	morning – mourning
border – boarder	muscle – mussel
bore – boar	navel – naval
born – borne	night – knight
bridle – bridal	patients – patience
bury – berry	pedal – peddle
caught – court	presents – presence
cereal – serial	principle – principal
council – counsel	profit – prophet
due – dew	rite – right – write
formally – formerly	root – route
freeze – frieze	sight – site – cite
gamble – gambol	stationary – stationery
gilt – guilt	stork – stalk
great – grate	taught – taut
hanger – hangar	threw – through
him – hymn	time – thyme
holy – wholly	vain – vein – vane
key – quay	wait – weight
knead – need	wave – waive
idle – idol	weather – whether – wether
lane – lain	whale – wail
lesson – lessen	whose – who's
mare – mayor	wine – whine

him – hymn

mussel – muscle

IDIOMS

Idioms are expressions or sayings that we sometimes use in friendly conversation. The meanings of these sayings have developed over many years. The meanings cannot be found in the words contained within them.

Many idioms had their origins in the Middle Ages. For example, 'to let the cat out of the bag' comes from the time cunning traders would swindle unsuspecting buyers by substituting a cat for a piglet. When the buyer got home and opened the bag a cat would jump out instead. People soon learned to always open the bag first before paying for the pig, thus exposing the trick.

Idiom	Meaning
to have an axe to grind	to take issue with something one feels strongly about
to have a bee in one's bonnet	to be possessed by a particular idea
to hit below the belt	to act unfairly towards a rival or an opponent
to be a wet blanket	to be a spoilsport
to have a bone to pick with someone	to have a dispute to settle or a complaint to make
to make a clean breast of it	to confess to some wrong doing
to take the bull by the horns	to meet difficulties or dangers boldly
to paddle one's own canoe	to do things for oneself
to put the cart before the horse	to do things the wrong way round
to be under a cloud	to be under suspicion
to make both ends meet	to have enough money to cover basic expenses
to have a feather in one's cap	to have done something to be proud of
to sit on the fence	to refuse to take sides in a dispute
to play second fiddle	to take a back seat while someone else leads
to bury the hatchet	to settle a quarrel and live in peace
to hang one's head	to be ashamed of oneself
to live from hand to mouth	to have only enough money to buy food to survive
to flog a dead horse	to do work which produces no results
to ride the high horse	to behave arrogantly; to be very haughty
to strike while the iron is hot	to act while conditions are favourable
to turn over a new leaf	to change habits and start living a new life
to make a mountain out of a molehill	to make trifling difficulties appear great ones
to face the music	to take punishment or criticism without complaint
to pay through the nose	to pay too high a price
to mind one's p's and q's	to be careful how one behaves
to smell a rat	to be suspicious
to give a person the cold shoulder	to ignore someone or make them feel unwelcome
to blow one's own trumpet	to boast about oneself
to get into hot water	to get into trouble

IMAGERY

Imagery is descriptive language used to evoke particular mental pictures. The words create sensory images, figures or likenesses of things. Imagery may be enhanced by the use of metaphors or similes. *(See Metaphors; Similes)*

INDEXES

The index of a book is a detailed alphabetical key to topics in the book with reference to their page number. Example:

Index

saccharia 11	snakes 46	table tennis 58
saints 17	solar system 50	tarantulas 64
salmon 26	submarine 52	telecommunications 68

The word 'index' is from Latin, meaning anything that shows or points out. The forefinger is called the index finger because it is used to indicate or point things out.

Just as a dictionary is a guide to the words in a language, an index is a guide to the contents of a book. The first word of each entry in an index is known as the catchword. When the subject of the entry is more than one word, the main one is made the catchword. When indexing the names of people the surname is always placed first. Thus you would look for *Adolf Hitler* under *H* not *A*. If you wanted to find information about wild rabbits you would turn to rabbits not wild. Subheadings are often given to make our search easier.

Example:

Rabbits
angora 36, 146
domestic 29, 36, 140–6
wild 147

An index also includes **cross-references** to draw attention to information supplied under other headings. For example, the entry *vehicles* may end with *See also – utilities, buses, four-wheel drives.*

INDIRECT SPEECH

Speech can be reported directly or indirectly.

Indirect speech reports a person's speech as part of the

narrative. It gives the gist of what has been said, but does not necessarily quote the exact words used. Therefore quotation marks are not needed.

Example:

Direct speech: *'I scored a goal,' said Paul to Steve.*

Indirect speech: *Paul told Steve that he had scored a goal.*

Indirect speech can be reported by a third person, as in the example above, but can also be reported by the speaker, or in the first person. Example: *I told Steve that I had scored a goal.* (Paul reporting what he said.)

INFERENCING

An inference is a calculated guess made on the basis of information that has been presented. When you make an inference it is important to decide whether you have enough information to make an accurate, or at least reasonable, guess.

This group of facts is followed by a number of inferences. In the space after each one write:

- **I**   if it is a calculated guess
- **T**   if it is definitely true
- **F**   if it is false
- **NEI**   if there is not enough information to make an accurate inference.

TRY THIS

To be able to live in Bentaland you must have blonde hair and blue eyes. Heidi and Joanne both have blonde hair and blue eyes. Michael has brown eyes and blonde hair. Sally wants to live in Australia for the rest of her life. Michael and Joanne are brother and sister and Sally is an only child.

a) Joanne wants to emigrate to Bentaland.   _____

b) Heidi and Joanne are close friends.   _____

c) Sally would like to live in Bentaland.   _____

d) Michael cannot live in Bentaland.   _____

e) Michael and Joanne would like to live
   in the same country.   _____

INTENSIFIERS

Intensifiers are adverbs that are used to strengthen or reinforce a message. Some examples include: *very, really, extremely, entirely, wholly, unusually, absolutely.*

Compare   *I am fairly sure she was quite pleased with the present.*
with   *I am absolutely sure she was immensely pleased with the present.*

The second sentence, which uses intensifiers, sounds much more genuine and convincing than the first sentence.

We use intensifiers to make our opinion clear. They are often used when trying to persuade others to see our point of view, when arguing or debating, when making a complaint or in advertising or reviews. *(See also Modality; Modifiers)*

INTERJECTION

Interjections are short exclamations that express strong feelings. They have no grammatical value.
When inserted into a sentence, an interjection has no grammatical connection to the rest of the sentence.

Examples: *Wow!   Aha!   Good grief!   Oh!*

JARGON

Many activities, ranging from professions to sports, have associated with them a jargon or special vocabulary. Doctors will know what is meant by 'Stat', 'CAT scan' or 'Code Blue'. AFL fans will understand the terms 'a six pointer', 'the pack fly for the ball' and 'he took a screamer'. Cricketers will know all about a 'wrong un', a 'long-hop', 'stealing a quick single' and 'getting a ton'.

Jargon is often undistinguishable from slang. Modern teenagers enjoy using their own jargon – a language familiar only to those belonging to a particular group.

TRY THIS

Write some original terms used only by you and your friends.

LEGENDS

Legends are stories handed down from generation to generation within a particular culture. Legends are popularly believed to have a historical basis, but are unable to be verified.

The word *legend* comes from the French word *legenda*, meaning 'to be read', and referred only to written stories, not to traditional stories passed on orally.

LETTER PATTERNS

Common letter patterns occur in many words. Studying and remembering these patterns helps us to strengthen our spelling and vocabulary skills. In English, many words are not spelt the way they sound, so it is important to remember the visual patterns of their letters.

Examples: *square, prepare, fare, parent; camel, lame, camera*

LITERATURE

Literature refers to novels, stories, poems and plays that entertain, inform, stimulate or provide artistic pleasure. It can also refer to an entire body of writing from a particular culture, time period or subject matter, eg medieval literature.

METAPHORS

Metaphors are used to make prose or poetry more colourful. We form metaphors by saying something is something else. Example: The **lawn** was a **carpet of green**.

The first verse of the poem 'The Highwayman' by Alfred Noyes has three metaphors. Can you find each one?

The wind was a torrent of darkness among the gusty trees.

The moon was a ghostly galleon tossed upon cloudy seas,

The road was a ribbon of moonlight over the purple moor,

And the highwayman came riding—

Riding—riding—

And the highwayman came riding up to the old inn door.

TRY THIS

M

MNEMONICS

Mnemonics are memory keys we can use to remember certain things. They may help you remember the spelling of difficult words, or the order of items in a list.

Examples:

calendar *has **da** at the end like **day**.*

separate *this word has 'a **rat** in it'.*

Saturday *is the day **ur** (you are) glad to see come because there is no school.*

stationery *has an **e** as in **letter**; stationary has an **a** as in **car**.*

The order of the planets:

My **V**ery **E**xcellent **M**other **J**ust **S**erved **U**s **N**oodles

(Mercury, Venus, Earth, Mars, Jupiter, Saturn, Uranus, Neptune)

MODALITY

When conversing with others we often add words to modify what we say because we may be uncertain, or to intensify our message if we have definite opinions. We can also add certain words simply to be well mannered and to make sure we get on well with others. This is known as modality and modulation.

Words called **modals** can be introduced into our conversations to show:

Certainty   How certain we are about something.
definitely, probably, might, maybe, possibly
Example: *I'll **definitely** be there. I **might** be there.*

Usuality   How often something happens.
always, sometimes, often, seldom, rarely
Example: *He **always** helps me. He **seldom** helps.*

Obligation   How much obligation we place on others.
must, should, can, could, ought
Example: *You **must** go now. You **ought** to go now.*

We often modify the directness of requests and suggestions we make by changing our wording. Between the directive to DO something and NOT DO something, there is a whole range of intensity options from which to choose. This is called modulation.

(See also Intensifiers; Modifiers)

MODERN WORDS

English is a growing language and new words are constantly being created to name new discoveries, inventions and technologies.

Here are some words that have been invented in the last hundred years: *microchip, transistor, polyester, heliport, synthetic, microsurgery, supersonic, fax, byte, disco.*

MODIFIERS

Modifiers are adverbs that are used to weaken or soften a message. Some examples include: *fairly, nearly, almost, quite, somewhat, rather, possibly, probably.*

Compare: *The book was long and boring.*
  with   *The book was **quite** long and **fairly** boring.*

The second sentence, which uses modifiers, doesn't make the book sound quite as hard to tackle as the first sentence.

(See also Intensifiers; Modality)

MOOD

When we write or speak we express mood through the sentence types we use. These are:

• statements   • commands   • questions

Declarative mood is expressed through statements. When we write a statement it begins with a capital letter and ends with a full stop (period).

Example: *We saw Tom in Melbourne.*

Statements can be either **fact** or **opinion**.

Examples: *A kangaroo is a marsupial.* (fact)
          Kangaroos are Australia's favourite animal. (opinion)

Imperative mood is expressed through commands or orders and is used to give instructions, orders or directions.

Examples: *(You) Mix the paints well.* (You = subject implied)

Interrogative mood is expressed through questions. When we write a question we begin with a capital letter and end in a question mark (?).

Examples: *Where is Tom?   What is your favourite food?*

Tag questions are written as statements with a tag at the end.

Examples: *That dog is yours, isn't it?*

You will help me, won't you?

Rhetorical questions are questions where an answer is not expected. Example: *Me? Sing by myself? Are you crazy?*

MORPHOLOGY

Morphology is centred around word structure. **Morphemes** are *affixes* and *root words*.

There are two types of morphemes.

Free (or unbound) morphemes are words, or parts of words, that can stand on their own.

Example: the word *seaweed* consists of two free or unbound morphemes *sea* and *weed*.

Bound morphemes cannot stand on their own. They must unite with free morphemes to make sense.

Example: the word *impossible* consists of the prefix *im*, which is a bound morpheme, and *possible*, a free morpheme.

Bound morphemes include:

- prefixes and suffixes **un**well and gold**en**
- possession   *The dog**'s** bone.*
- tense markers   *He is jok**ing**. The cattle stray**ed**.*
- inflection   *We played in the bush**es**.*
- agreement in person
  and number   *The dog bark**s**.*

MYTHS

A myth is a special kind of story about gods, heroes and other supernatural beings or creatures. Great myths have been created by the Egyptians, Persians, Japanese, Chinese, Indigenous Australians, Native Americans, Indians and most other cultures around the world. Some words we use today have their origins in myths. For example: *atlas*, a book of maps, gets its name from the Ancient Greek myth about a god named Atlas, who was forced to hold the world and sky on his shoulders.

NAMES

We have two kinds of names: (1) a given or first name, which is chosen for us by our parents; and (2) a family name or surname, which is usually the same as our father's.

Sometimes we are also given a nickname by our friends. 'Nickname' comes from the Middle English word 'ekename', which meant an additional name.

English family names have developed in many ways. They were often given to describe:

- Where a person lived.
  eg: *Peter of the Woodlands = Peter Woods*

- A person's occupation.
  eg: *Michael the Butcher = Michael Butcher*

- What a person looked like or features they had.
  eg: *Armstrong, Brown, Longfellow, Short*

- Some names were passed on. Example: In England, Joe the son of Peter became known as *Joe Peterson*. In Scotland, the prefix Mac or Mc meant 'son of', so *Jack McDonald* meant Jack, son of Donald.

- Survey your classmates to see from what countries their names come and know how their names began.

- Many people change their names. For example Elton John's original name was Reginald Dwight. If you could change your name, what would you change it to, and why?

- A music teacher had the name *Mrs Screech*. Think up some more humorous names for certain occupations, for example, a doctor whose family name is *Pain*.

Little naked bush cherubs with gumnut hats, Snugglepot and Cuddlepie were the creation of May Gibbs, who was born in England and migrated with her parents to Western Australia as a child in 1881.

TRY THIS

NEOLOGISMS

A neologism is a word or phrase that has recently come into use, or a new meaning or usage given to an existing word or phrase.

Examples: *to impact, to update, ongoing, input, downsize*
Neologism usually has negative connotations and is applied to words considered jargon, unclear or too unusual. Once the word is accepted into the language it is no longer called a neologism.

People often avoid using neologisms in writing.
When considering such words ask yourself: Is the word necessary or useful? Does the word suit the idea it is attempting to convey?

NOMINALISATION

Nominalisation is the process by which we form nouns from other parts of speech.

Examples:

Verb: speak – *speech*

Verb: persuade – *persuasion*

Adjective: golden – *gold*

Adjective: beautiful – *beauty*

Adjective: flexible – *flexibility*

Verb: lose – *loss*

Adjective: strong – *strength*

Adjective: honest – *honesty*

NOUNS (NAMING WORDS)

Nouns are the names of things around us.

There are different types of nouns.

Common nouns are used to name general things, rather than a particular person or thing.

Examples: *cat, chair, bicycle, book, girl, tree*

Proper nouns are the names of specific people, places, days, months and special events. They are written with a capital letter at the beginning. Example: *Nicole Kidman* stayed at the *Hilton Hotel* in *Adelaide* last *July*.

Collective nouns are the names we use for collections of things.

Examples: a *flock* of sheep, a *herd* of cattle, a *pack* of dogs, a *bunch* of bananas, a *smack* of jellyfish, a *murder* of crows, an *army* of frogs, a *charm* of finches, a *pod* of whales

Other collective nouns name a number of different things in the same class. Examples: *tools, diseases, luggage, fruit, pasta*

Terms of address are the nouns we use when we refer to or address certain people. Examples: *Mr* Jones   *Ms* Smith   *Doctor* Rhodes   *Captain* Peters

Abstract nouns name things that can't be recognised by the five senses – you can't touch, taste, hear, smell or see them – they can only be recognised by the mind, such as moods and emotions.

Examples: *courage, misery, delight, fear, happiness, excitement, distress, hope, hunger, possibility*

It is important to understand the relationship of nouns to other words such as verbs (words that tell what the noun is doing), adjectives (words that describe the noun) and pronouns (words that take the place of a noun).

Common Noun Examples

Animals: armadillo, alligator, antelope, bandicoot, echidna, crocodile, reindeer, porpoise, squirrel, platypus, deer, puma

Birds: albatross, pelican, sparrow, plover, kookaburra, cockatoo, lorikeet, crow, wagtail, duck, eagle, buzzard

Insects: locust, grasshopper, aphid, mosquito, louse, weevil, wasp, hornet, tse-tse fly, blowfly, flea, butterfly

Tools: pliers, scissors, hammer, nails, ramp, screwdriver, chisel, plane, jigsaw, tape-measure, hand-saw

In the garden: flowers, hose, spray, manure, hoe, shovel, shrub, bush, plants, vegetables, insecticide, furrow, seeds, gloves

At school: classroom, teacher, pencil, television, computer, principal, gymnasium, canteen, parent, student, desk, whiteboard

Proper Noun Examples

Countries: Australia, Vietnam, England, Wales, Scotland, Ireland, China, Canada, United States, Malaysia, France, Gambia, Indonesia, Iran, Iraq, Jamaica, Denmark, East Timor, Brazil, Japan, Spain, Sweden, Austria, Belgium, Cuba

Cities: London, Sydney, Melbourne, Adelaide, Perth, Brisbane, Hobart, Amsterdam, Athens, Auckland, Beijing, Berlin, Bombay, Cairo, Chicago, Paris, Dublin, Edinburgh, Manila, Jerusalem, Baghdad, Jakarta, Frankfurt, Venice, Moscow, Toronto, Port Moresby, Dili

Languages: Afrikaans, Arabic, Mandarin, Cantonese, Croatian, English, Filipino, Finnish, Flemish, Hebrew, Hindi, Icelandic, Italian, Japanese, Khmer, Kurdish, Maori, Russian, Samoan, Swahili, Thai, Turkish, Urdu, Vietnamese, Welsh

Celebrations/Special Times: Anzac Day, All Saints Day, Bastille Day, Boxing Day, Chinese New Year, Christmas Eve, Easter, Halloween, Hanukkah, Yom Kippur, May Day, Melbourne Cup, Remembrance Day, St Valentine's Day, Ramadan, Thanksgiving, Waitangi Day

Terms of Address:

Captain, Dame, Sir, Doctor (Dr), Father, Reverend, Ms, Mr, Mrs, Lady, Lord, Judge/Justice, Master, Your Highness, Your Honour, Your Worship

Abstract Nouns Examples

affection, hope, love, despair, sadness, joy, beauty, kindness, greed, avarice, anger, danger, dismay, peril, pleasure, laziness, imagination, distress, failure, excitement, gladness, boredom, confidence, experience, loneliness, satisfaction, honesty, fun, joy, delight, shame, possibility

Collective Nouns Examples

assembly, bouquet, committee, class, convoy, congregation, organisation, quiver, barren (mules), flock (birds, sheep), bevy (quail), gaggle (geese), skein (geese in flight), game (swans), host (sparrows), kennel (hounds), kindle (kittens), kit (pigeons), muster (peacocks), shoal (fish), skulk (foxes), sleuth (bears), tiding (magpies), unkindness (ravens), wedge (swans in flight)

NOUNS FROM VERBS

Nouns can be formed from verbs. Making nouns from other parts of speech is called nominalisation.

Verb	Noun	Verb	Noun	Verb	Noun
abolish	abolition	compel	compulsion	explore	exploration
accept	acceptance	compensate	compensation	expose	exposure
accompany	accompaniment	complain	complaint	extend	extension
accuse	accusation	complete	completion	fly	flight
acquaint	acquaintance	compose	composition	grieve	grief
act	action	confide	confidence	grow	growth
admit	admission	confuse	confusion	hate	hatred
adopt	adoption	congratulate	congratulation	hinder	hindrance
advertise	advertisement	conspire	conspiracy	imagine	imagination
advise	advice	construct	construction	imitate	imitation
allow	allowance	converse	conversation	inform	information
appear	appearance	correct	correction	injure	injury
applaud	applause	create	creation	inquire	inquiry
apply	application	deceive	deceit	intend	intention
approve	approval	decide	decision	interfere	interference
arrive	arrival	declare	declaration	introduce	introduction
ascend	ascent	defend	defence	invade	invasion
assist	assistance	defy	defiance	invent	invention
attract	attraction	deliver	delivery	invite	invitation
begin	beginning	depart	departure	judge	judgment
behave	behaviour	depend	dependence	know	knowledge
believe	belief	describe	description	laugh	laughter
betray	betrayal	destroy	destruction	lose	loss
bore	boredom	discover	discovery	manage	management
calculate	calculation	disturb	disturbance	marry	marriage
cancel	cancellation	divide	division	mock	mockery
choose	choice	encourage	encouragement	move	movement
circulate	circulation	enter	entrance	obey	obedience
clean	cleanliness	exclaim	exclamation	obstruct	obstruction
clear	clearance	exhaust	exhaustion	occupy	occupation
collect	collection	exist	existence	occur	occurrence
combine	combination	expect	expectation	oppose	opposition
commence	commencement	expel	expulsion	organise	organisation
communicate	communication	explain	explanation	perform	performance
compare	comparison	explode	explosion	permit	permission

Verb	Noun	Verb	Noun	Verb	Noun
persuade	*persuasion*	prosecute	*prosecution*	resist	*resistance*
please	*pleasure*	prosper	*prosperity*	resolve	*resolution*
portray	*portrayal*	prove	*proof*	reveal	*revelation*
postpone	*postponement*	pursue	*pursuit*	revise	*revision*
practise	*practice*	qualify	*qualification*	revive	*revival*
prepare	*preparation*	rebel	*rebellion*	revolve	*revolution*
press	*pressure*	receive	*receipt*	satisfy	*satisfaction*
prescribe	*prescription*	recognise	*recognition*	seize	*seizure*
pretend	*pretence*	reduce	*reduction*	serve	*service*
prevail	*prevalence*	relieve	*relief*	sever	*severance*
proceed	*procedure*	rely	*reliance*	subscribe	*subscription*
proclaim	*proclamation*	remain	*remainder*	succeed	*success*
produce	*production*	repeat	*repetition*	tempt	*temptation*
pronounce	*pronunciation*	resemble	*resemblance*	think	*thought*
prophesy	*prophecy*	reside	*residence*	translate	*translation*
propose	*proposal*	resign	*resignation*	transmit	*transmission*

NUANCE

A nuance is a subtle or slight degree of difference in the meaning or feeling of something expressed. It is from the French, meaning 'shades of colour'. So it could refer to a hint of sadness underlying the words of a poem, or the impression of anger given in the delivery of lines in a play.

Examples:

The original nuance of the poem was lost in the translation.

Her performance in the play explored every emotional nuance.

NUMBER

When a noun refers to just one thing it is said to be **singular**. When the number referred to is more than one it is said to be **plural**. Here are some helpful rules to remember when forming plurals:

- Most nouns form their plural by adding **s**, eg the plural of *boy* is *boys*.
- Nouns ending in **ch**, **sh**, **s** or **x** add **es** to form their plural, eg *dish – dishes, church – churches, box – boxes*.
- Nouns ending in **y**, before which there is a vowel, simply add **s** to form their plural, eg *monkey – monkeys*.
- Nouns ending in **y**, before which there is a consonant, form their plural by changing the **y** to **i** and adding **es**, eg *bunny – bunnies*.
- Some nouns ending in **f** form their plurals by changing the **f** to **v** and adding **es**, eg *leaf – leaves*. However, not all nouns ending in **f** follow this rule, eg *roof – roofs*.
- The plural of nouns ending in **o** is formed by either adding **s**, eg *piano – pianos*, or by adding **es**, eg *cargo – cargoes*.
- Some nouns form their plural by changing a vowel or adding **en**, eg *foot – feet, ox – oxen*.
- The plurals of some compound words are formed by adding **s** to the first word, eg *brother-in-law – brother**s**-in-law*.

OBJECTS

In a sentence, the object is the person or thing affected by the action of a verb. Objects can be affected directly or indirectly. Example:

- Directly *I ate **the cake***.
- Indirectly *I gave **her** a present.*

All sentences have a subject, but may not have an object.

ONOMATOPOEIA

Onomatopoeia is a formation of a word by imitating a sound associated with the subject. It is also known as **echoism**, as the sound produced in saying the word reflects the actual sound made. Such words are most effective when they are read out loud. Examples: *crash, bang, whiz, fizz, hiss, plop, snort, splash, toot toot, moo, ding-a-ling, clip-clop, purr, prang*

The words used to describe the sounds that animals make are onomatopoeic. Different countries choose different words to describe these sounds. For example, we use *quack quack* for the noise of a duck. In France, ducks say *coin coin*. In Finland, *kvaak kvaak*. In Denmark, *rap rap*. In Mexico, *cua cua*. In Japan, *ga ga*.

TRY THIS

Make up your own onomatopoeic words. ⬅

Onomatopoeia Examples

boing	fizz	pop	splash
boom	flap	prang	splutter
buzz	gulp	puff	squelch
chirp	gurgle	quack	tick
clang	hiss	rattle	twitter
click	kerdoink	rip	whirr
clunk	mumble	roar	whiz
crack	oink	scratch	whoosh
crackle	ooze	screech	zap
crash	pitter patter	slop	zip
creak	plonk	smack	zoom
cuckoo	plop	snap	

Note: Most onomatopoeic words are original and have no history, no etymology. They are root words created to represent a sound. This is probably how the first sounds made by people came into existence. They are still being created today, like *prang* to represent the sound of crashing vehicles.

OXYMORON

An oxymoron is a figure of speech that uses two contradictory terms. It comes from the Greek word meaning 'sharply dull' or 'pointedly foolish'.

Examples: *soft rock   bitter sweet   cruel to be kind*

PALINDROMES

Palindromes are words or sentences which are spelt the same way both forwards and backwards. Examples:

bib	eye	minim	pop
did	gag	mum	pup
dad	gig	nan	radar
deed	Hannah	noon	redder
dud	Glenelg	peep	refer
eve	level	pep	
ewe	madam	pip	

The Guinness Book of Records lists the word redivider as the longest palindromic word in English.

Palindromic sentences include:

Madam I'm Adam.
No devils lived on.
Was it a rat I saw?
Able was I ere I saw Elba.

A man, a plan, a canal, Panama.
Moor as a hobo has a room.
Did Dad say as Dad did?

(Attributed to Napoleon Bonaparte when his French army was defeated and he was imprisoned on the Isle of Elba.)

PARABLES

A parable is a short story that teaches a moral lesson. In the Bible, there are many parables told by Jesus Christ. *(See also Fables)*

PARADOX

A paradox is a saying or a situation which seems to contradict itself; it's apparent nonsense, however, emphasises a truth.

Example: *More haste, less speed.*

This paradox means that if you rush something, you are much more likely to make mistakes and have to start again, taking longer to complete the task than if you had gone more carefully in the first place.

There is a famous paradox called the **liar's paradox**. It is the simple sentence: *This sentence is a lie.*

- If the sentence is true, then it is a lie, as it says. But if it is a lie, how can it be true? A lie cannot also be the truth. So the sentence being true makes it a lie.

- If the sentence is a lie, then it is not as it says, it is true. So the sentence being a lie makes it true.

PARAGRAPHS

A paragraph is a group of sentences that form a logical unit, where each idea relates to the same purpose. The main idea of a paragraph is normally stated in a single sentence often called a **topic sentence**. This is often the first sentence, but may occur anywhere in the paragraph.

Conventions in writing paragraphs

Paragraphs always begin on a new line.

The first word of each paragraph may begin a little way in from the margin. This is called indentation or indenting the paragraph. Alternatively, a line space can be left between paragraphs with no indentation.

Each sentence should relate closely to the topic sentence, providing additional information to support the main idea. The link between each sentence should be clear. Linking words are very important and help the sentences to flow on from one another. Some useful linking words are:

since	again	however	all in all
similarly	finally	nevertheless	in conclusion
also	likewise	in addition	therefore
besides	although	for example	in short

The length of paragraphs is also important. Paragraphs that are too long can be boring and the reader will lose interest, while paragraphs that are too short may seem jerky and disjointed. Sometimes, however, short paragraphs can be used to create a sense of action and excitement.

When writing dialogue, each new speaker should start a new paragraph.

PARODY

A parody is a humorous, often exaggerated, imitation of a serious literary work.

PARTICIPLES

A participle is a form taken by a verb to indicate tense (when the action takes place). All verbs have two participle forms: past and present.

The **present participle** is formed by adding **ing** to the base verb:

wish – wishing   leave – leaving   go – going   run – running

The **past participle** is usually formed by adding **d**, **ed** or **t** to the base verb: *wished hoped drowned shopped leapt*

There are also many verbs that have irregular past participles.

Verb	Past Participle	Verb	Past Participle
catch	*caught*	run	*ran*
do	*done*	ring	*rung*
forget	*forgotten*	think	*thought*

Auxiliary verbs

Notice that a participle always needs a helping word such as *is, was, were, has, have, had*. These are called **auxiliary verbs**. The regular past tense form does not require a helping word.

Example:

(a) *The girl ate the cake.*   (b) *The cake was eaten by the girl.*

In (a) the word *ate* is the past tense of *eat*. In (b) the word *eaten* is the past participle of *eat*, and requires the auxiliary verb *was*.

(See also Auxiliary Verbs)

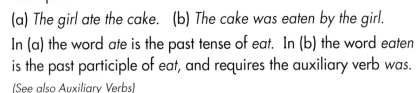

PERSON

A pronoun has three different forms. They are:

- **First person** refers to the person who is speaking.
  Examples: ***I*** *am running.* ***We*** *are here.*

- **Second person** refers to the person being spoken to.
  Example: ***You*** *must not be late.*

- **Third person** refers to the person being spoken about.
  Examples: ***He*** *is ill.* ***She*** *has arrived.* ***They*** *are late.*

	Singular	*Plural*
First person	I, me	we, us
Second person	you	you
Third person	he, she, it, him, her	they, them

(See also Pronouns)

PERSONIFICATION

Personification is a type of imagery where animals or inanimate objects are given human characteristics, feelings or actions.
Examples:
The tree beckoned me outside and shivered as the wind whispered secrets through her leaves.
The injured car took one last shuddering breath then died.

PHRASES

A phrase is a group of words that add detail to a sentence. They do not have a subject or finite verb, so can only make sense within a sentence.

Example: *The girl **with red hair** won the race.*

There are different types of phrases that do the same job as other parts of speech.

Adjectival phrases do the work of an adjective. They tell us more about a noun or pronoun. They should be placed close to the noun they are describing.

Example: *The man **with black hair** hit the ball.*

Adverbial phrases do the work of an adverb. They tell us more about the action of the verb by adding detail about how, when, where, why or for how long something is happening or has happened.

Example: *I was stuck in traffic **for two hours**.* (for how long)
*We walked **to the bus stop**.* (where)
*The boy kicked the ball **with great skill**.* (how)

Noun phrases or **Noun groups** do the work of a noun. They answer the question 'What?'.

Examples: ***Playing football** requires a lot of skill.*
    ***The result of the test** is still not known.*

Prepositional phrases do the work of an adjective or an adverb. They answer the questions 'Which one?' or 'How?', 'When?' or 'Where?'.

Examples: *The towel **on the floor** is wet.*
    (Which towel? The one on the floor.)
    *I found my keys **behind the couch**.*
    (Where were the keys? Behind the couch.)

POETRY

Poetry is a very different text type. The purpose of poetry or verse is to capture the emotion of an event or some object or a person. Words are connected, but not always in grammatically correct sentences. They are linked by meaning and emotion. Poetic language often rhymes, or has a natural rhythm that is best captured when read aloud.

Each type of poetry has its own structure and organisation. The different forms of poetry include:

Acrostics

In this type of poem we write the topic of the poem down the left side of the page. Each line begins with the first letter of the topic or chosen word. There is no title.

Example: **M** *ischievous little creatures playing all day*

   I *n the pantry or the kitchen*

   C *ats like to catch you*

   E *ating the scraps I throw away*

Ballads

A ballad is a poem, often meant to be sung, that tells a story.

Examples: *The Highwayman* by Alfred Noyes

   The Wild Colonial Boy by A.B. 'Banjo' Patterson

Cinquain

In this type of poem we begin with a title, which is the topic. There are five lines. Line 1 = 2 syllables, Line 2 = 4 syllables, Line 3 = 6 syllables, Line 4 = 8 syllables, Line 5 = 2 syllables with a twist or surprise comment.

Example:

Title	**Dogs**
Line 1	Big dogs
Line 2	Mischievous dogs
Line 3	Pups, bones, barking and more
Line 4	Fetching sticks and rolling over
Line 5	Big ears

Couplets

Couplets are two successive lines of poetry, which usually rhyme.

Example: *A robin redbreast in a cage*

   Puts all of heaven in a rage.

Make up your own rhyming couplet. It can be humorous or serious.

TRY THIS

Free Verse

Free verse is a poem without regular meter or line length. It has a title, followed by a single stanza with 5 lines. It usually has a circular pattern, meaning the first and last lines are related.
Example:

> ### Frost
>
> *Can you imagine frost*
> *Setting on the grass*
> *Cold and chilly on your cheeks*
> *Freezing all the ground*
> *Just imagine, frost.*

Haiku

Haiku is a three line poem that does not rhyme.
Line 1 = 5 syllables, Line 2 = 7 syllables, and Line 3 = 5 syllables.
Haiku originated in Japan and expresses the strong sensations of a moment in sharp images.
Example:

> ### Winter
>
> *Fiercely lashing trees*
> *Dropping leaves as branches sway*
> *Invisible cold.*

PORTMANTEAU WORDS

Portmanteau words are made by joining part of one word to part of another in order to convey the ideas behind both words.

The term was coined by Lewis Carroll, who is famous for making up such words. He invented the word *chortle*, which joined the words 'chuckle' and 'snort'. In his book *Through the Looking Glass*, the character of Humpty Dumpty explains '…it's like a *portmanteau* [a type of suitcase] – there are two meanings packed up into one word'.

Some common portmanteau words include:

newscast	from news and broadcast
smog	from smoke and fog
Medicare	from medical and care
brunch	from breakfast and lunch
melodrama	from melody and drama
never	from not and ever
motel	from motor and hotel
smash	from smack and bash
breathalyser	from breath and analyser
flare	from flash and glare
heliport	from helicopter and airport
telecast	from television and broadcast
paratroops	from parachute and troops
twirl	from twist and swirl
glimmer	from glare and shimmer
moped	from motor and pedal
squiggle	from squirm and wriggle

moped

PREFIXES

A prefix is a syllable added to the front of a base word. It is often used to change a word to one of opposite meaning.

When adding a prefix, no spelling changes have to be made. You simply add the prefix.

Example: *in + visible = invisible   un + necessary = unnecessary*

Prefixes are usually derived from Latin, Greek or Old English words. The lists below show the literal meanings of common prefixes.

Old English Prefixes

be (to make) – befriend

for (negative) – forbid

mis (wrong) – mistake

off (from) – offspring

over (over) – overdo

un (not) – unfair

un (reverse) – unclench

with (back, against) – withdraw

Latin Prefixes

ab (away from) – abduct

bene (well) – benefit

bi (twice) – bicycle

contra (against) – contradict

dis (negative) – disappear

ex (out of) – explode

ob (against) – object

sub (under) – submarine

Greek Prefixes

anti (against) – antiseptic	mono (single) – monopoly
auto (self) – autograph	poly (many) – polygon
dia (through) – diameter	phil (love of) – philosophy
homo (same) – homophone	tele (from afar) – television

PREPOSITIONS

Prepositions are words we use to show the relationship of a noun or a pronoun to another word in the sentence. They can be called 'place words' because they often tell us the position of things.

Examples:

*The puppy is **on** the chair.* *The puppy is **beside** the chair.*
*The puppy is **under** the chair.* *The puppy is **between** the chairs.*

Examples:

aboard	below	inside	through
about	beneath	into	to
above	beside	near	towards
across	between	of	under
after	beyond	off	underneath
against	by	on	until
along	despite	onto	up
among	down	opposite	upon
around	during	outside	with
at	except	over	within
away	for	past	without
before	from	round	
behind	in	since	

Things to beware of when using prepositions:

- **among / between** Something is shared *among* several people (three or more). Something is shared *between* two people.

  Examples: *I shared the cake **among** the whole class.*

  *I shared the cake **between** Mary and myself.*

- **in / into** *In* shows position in one place. *Into* shows movement from one place to another.

  Examples: *The teacher is **in** the room.*

  *The boy dived **into** the river.*

- **different from** One thing or person is *different from* another. Never say different *than*.

- **beside / besides** *Beside* means at the side of. *Besides* means in addition to.

  Examples: *The teacher stood* **beside** *the table.*
  Several girls were there **besides** *Rani.*

Preposition or adverb?

Some prepositions may look like adverbs. To tell whether the word is a preposition or an adverb, look at the way it is used. If it is describing the position of a noun or pronoun, it is a preposition. Look at the following sentences.

I fell **down**.

Down is a place word. It tells where I (pronoun) fell.

A boat sailed **under** *the bridge.*

Under is a preposition. It tells the position of the boat (noun).

A preposition usually has a noun or pronoun after it.

PRONOUNS

Pronouns are used to take the place of nouns. By using pronouns we can talk about people or things without naming them every time. This helps prevent our speech or writing from becoming disjointed because of too much repetition. Without pronouns we would have to write:

Bill said that Bill couldn't come because Bill's mother hadn't bought Bill a new pair of sneakers.

Using pronouns we can write:

Bill said that **he** *couldn't come because* **his** *mother hadn't bought* **him** *a new pair of sneakers.*

There are different types of pronouns.

Personal pronouns

	Subjective		Objective	
	Singular	**Plural**	**Singular**	**Plural**
First person	I	we	me	us
Second person	you	you	you	you
Third person	he, she, it	they	him, her, it	them

Things to remember:

- If a pronoun is the subject or part of the subject of a sentence, it is in the **subjective** case.

  Example: **She** *is coming to my house.*

- If a pronoun is the object or indirect object of a sentence, it is in the **objective** case.
  Examples: *We saw **them** at the zoo.*   *I gave **him** the book.*

- **First person pronouns** are used if we are talking about ourselves. Examples: *I am nine years old.*
  We are learning about sharks.

- The **second person pronoun** is used if we are talking to someone. Example: *Are **you** going to be long?*

- **Third person pronouns** are used if we are talking about someone or something else.
  Examples: ***She** was late for school.   **They** arrived by bus.*
  ***It** was on the table.*

Possessive pronouns

	Singular	**Plural**
First person	my mine	our ours
Second person	your yours	your yours
Third person	his her hers its	their theirs

Possessive pronouns show ownership.

Examples: *This is **my** pen.   Here is **your** hat.*
*The cat licked **its** paw.*

Relative pronouns not only take the place of nouns but also help join sentences. The main relative pronouns are: *who, whom, whose, which, that.*

- **Who** and **whom** are used to refer to people. *Who* is subjective case and is used when referring to the subject of the verb. *Whom* is objective case and used when referring to the subject of the verb.
  Examples: *The girl **who** wore the blue hat.*
  *The friend with **whom** I went to the park.*

- **Which** and **that** are used to refer to animals, places and things.

Interrogative pronouns ask questions.

Examples: **Who** *paid?* **What** *is that?*

Other interrogative pronouns are: *whom, whose, which.*

Demonstrative pronouns (sometimes called determiners)
are used to stand for and point out nouns.
Examples: *That* toy belongs to Katy. *This* toy belongs to me.
Those boxes were taken away. *These* boxes were left behind.

Indefinite pronouns stand for a person, place or thing which
is not particularly defined.
Example: *Is **anyone** interested in football?*

Other indefinite pronouns are:

one	*none*	*somebody*	*everyone*
someone	*everything*	*anybody*	*anything*
no-one	*nobody*		

Problem pronouns

- **its / it's**

 Its is a pronoun that means belonging to *it*.
 Example: *The dog wagged **its** tail.*

 It's is not a pronoun. It is a contraction of *it is*.
 Example: ***It's** a friendly dog.*

- **I / me**

 Sometimes it is difficult to decide when to use *I* or *me* in
 a sentence. If in doubt, divide the sentence into two short
 sentences.

 > *Mike is going to the circus.*
 >
 > *I am going to the circus.*

 So the correct usage is: *Mike and **I** are going to the circus.*

 > *Jack told Sally to get off the grass.*
 >
 > *Jack told me to get off the grass.*

 So the correct usage is:
 > *Jack told Sally and **me** to get off the grass.*

PRONUNCIATION

Stress or Accent

If we are to pronounce a word correctly, we must be familiar with the sounds that go to make it, and we must also be aware of where the stress or accent falls. We must be able to break the word into syllables to determine the syllable on which the stress falls. Single-syllable words are generally easy but problems can occur with multi-syllable words.

Examples:

- Words of two syllables with the stress on the first syllable

  teach/er   **sis**/ter   **a**/gile

- Words of two syllables with the stress on the second syllable

  be/**gin**   ob/**scure**   be/**hind**

- Words of two syllables with both stressed.

  back/wards   arm/chair   thir/teen

- Words of three syllables with the stress on the first syllable

  su/i/cide   **lem**/on/ade   **el**/e/gant

- Words of three syllables with the stress on the second syllable

  de/**lic**/ious   sugg/**est**/ed   re/**hears**/al

- Words of three syllables with the stress on the third syllable

  dis/re/**gard**   mis/di/**rect**   in/dis/**creet**

- Words of four or more syllables usually, but not always, stress the third from last

  pho/**tog**/raph/er   i/**den**/tic/al

The importance of the position of the stress is evident when we see how words can change their meaning or function completely with a shift in the syllable to be stressed.

Examples:

con/tent (noun)	the information in a book
con/**tent** (adjective)	happy with what you have got
des/ert (noun)	sandy dry waste land
des/**ert** (verb)	to run away
min/ute (noun)	sixty seconds
min/**ute** (adjective)	very small
re/fuse (noun)	trash, garbage
re/**fuse** (verb)	to decline

PROVERBS

Proverbs, like adages, are wise sayings that have been in use for many years.

Absence makes the heart grow fonder.

Actions speak louder than words.

Beggars can't be choosers.

Early to bed, early to rise.

A bird in the hand is worth two in the bush.

Once bitten, twice shy.

You cannot get blood out of a stone.

New brooms sweep clean.

You can't have your cake and eat it too.

A cat may look at a king.

When the cat's away the mice will play.

Charity begins at home.

Don't count your chickens until they are hatched.

Every cloud has a silver lining.

Cut your coat according to your cloth.

Too many cooks spoil the broth.

Barking dogs seldom bite.

Let sleeping dogs lie.

A drowning man will clutch at a straw.

Don't put all your eggs in one basket.

Enough is as good as a feast.

Exchange is no robbery.

Fine feathers make fine birds.

Where there's smoke there's fire.

First come, first served.

A fool and his money are soon parted.

Fortune knocks once at every man's door.

A friend in need is a friend indeed.

Forbidden fruit tastes sweetest.

Out of the frying-pan into the fire.

God helps those who help themselves.

Grasp all, lose all.

Habit is second nature.

As well be hanged for a sheep as a lamb.

More haste, less speed.

Make hay while the sun shines.

Two heads are better than one.

Faint heart never won fair lady.

Honesty is the best policy.

Hunger is the best sauce.

Imitation is the sincerest form of flattery.

A pet lamb is a cross ram.

Better late than never.

He who laughs last laughs longest.

A small leak will sink a great ship.

Listeners hear no good of themselves.

Half a loaf is better than no bread.

Look before you leap.

One man's meat is another man's poison.

A miss is as good as a mile.

Necessity is the mother of invention.

No news is good news.

He who pays the piper calls the tune.

Little pitchers have long ears.

Any port in a storm.

Let not the pot call the kettle black.

Practice makes perfect.

Pride goes before a fall.

Robbing Peter to pay Paul.

What's sauce for the goose is sauce for the gander.

Out of sight, out of mind.

One swallow does not make a summer.

Set a thief to catch a thief.

Time and tide wait for no man.

Truth will out.

One good turn deserves another.

Empty vessels make the most noise.

Waste not, want not.

We never miss the water till the well runs dry.

All's well that ends well.

Leave well alone.

Where there's a will there's a way.

It's an ill wind that blows nobody any good.

All work and no play makes Jack a dull boy.

PUNCTUATION

Punctuation has been described as the 'traffic lights' of English. It plays an important role in our writing and reading.

To understand the importance of punctuation marks, read how the following marks can alter the entire meaning of a sentence.

(a) Have you eaten Billy?
(b) Have you eaten, Billy?
In which one is Billy on the menu?

(a) Michelle is a pretty, kind girl.
(b) Michelle is a pretty kind girl.
Which one would Michelle prefer?

(a) Sam said, 'I did it.'
(b) Sam said, 'I did it?'
(c) Sam said, 'I did it!'

(a) The boy called the teachers' names as they entered the hall.
(b) The boy called the teachers names as they entered the hall.
Which one shows the boy is rude?

(a) I played tennis with Mary James, Tom and Sue.
(b) I played tennis with Mary, James, Tom and Sue.
Which one tells us five people are playing tennis?

P

Apostrophe (')

Contractions

Apostrophes are used to mark shortened phrases called contractions. It shows where letters have been left out. Contractions are used in modern speech and in informal writing.

Here is a list of common contractions.

I am	*I'm*	we have	*we've*	what is	*what's*
I have	*I've*	we had	*we'd*	what has	*what's*
I had	*I'd*	we would	*we'd*	who is	*who's*
I would	*I'd*	we will	*we'll*	who has	*who's*
I will	*I'll*	let us	*let's*	who have	*who've*
you are	*you're*	could have	*could've*	who would	*who'd*
you have	*you've*	should have	*should've*	who will	*who'll*
you had	*you'd*	would have	*would've*	shall not	*shan't*
you would	*you'd*	here is	*here's*	will not	*won't*
you will	*you'll*	there is	*there's*	can not	*can't*
it is; it has	*it's*	there has	*there's*	could not	*couldn't*
it would	*it'd*	there had	*there'd*	do not	*don't*
it had	*it'd*	there would	*there'd*	does not	*doesn't*
it will	*it'll*	there will	*there'll*	did not	*didn't*
that is	*that's*	he is	*he's*	is not	*isn't*
that has	*that's*	he has	*he's*	has not	*hasn't*
that will	*that'll*	he had	*he'd*	have not	*haven't*
that had	*that'd*	he would	*he'd*	had not	*hadn't*
that would	*that'd*	he will	*he'll*	was not	*wasn't*
she is	*she's*	they are	*they're*	were not	*weren't*
she has	*she's*	they have	*they've*	has not	*hasn't*
she had	*she'd*	they had	*they'd*	have not	*haven't*
she would	*she'd*	they would	*they'd*	are not	*aren't*
she will	*she'll*	they will	*they'll*		
we are	*we're*	where is	*where's*		

Possession

Apostrophes are used with nouns to show ownership.

- The possessive of **singular nouns** is formed by adding an apostrophe and **s**.

  Examples: Harry**'s** lunch   the woman**'s** bag

  Grandpa**'s** beard   a mouse**'s** tail

  the ship**'s** cat   my dress**'s** zipper

- To make the possessive of **regular plural nouns**, just add an apostrophe.

  Examples: girls – girls**'**   ladies – ladies**'**

  glasses – glasses**'**

- The possessive of **irregular plural nouns** (not ending in **s**) is formed by adding an apostrophe and **s**. Do not change the spelling of the original word.

  Examples: women – women**'s**   men – men**'s**

  children – children**'s**

- To make the possessive of **proper nouns** of one syllable which **end in s**, add an apostrophe and **s**.

  Example: Jones**'s** bakery   Paris**'s** famous cafés

  Gus**'s** bike

- In **compound words**, add the apostrophe to the last word.

  Example: son-in-law**'s** house

- Where there are **several owners** of the same thing, only the last one mentioned gets an apostrophe.

  Examples: Anna and Jeremy**'s** dog

  Blaxland, Lawson and Wentworth**'s** expedition

- The possessive of Jesus is always Jesus**'**.

Brackets or parentheses ( )

Brackets are used for asides or for including additional information.

Example: Citrus fruits (oranges, lemons and limes) are rich in Vitamin C.

Colon (:)

- Colons may be used to introduce a list.

  Example: You will need: a pair of scissors; glue; a pen; a sheet of white paper.

- A colon is used to introduce a description, or elements of a set.

  Example: I have three sisters: Helen, Susie and Angela.

- To create a strong contrast.

  Example: *God creates: man destroys.*

- In play scripts, colons are used after each characters name, to introduce the words they will speak. Example: *GOLDILOCKS: Grandma, what big teeth you have!*

  WOLF: All the better to eat you with!

- Colons are used in dictionaries to introduce definitions and examples.

  Example: *A: the first letter of the English alphabet.*

- Some movie or book titles use a colon to separate the main title and a subtitle.

  Example: *Star Wars Episode IV: A New Hope*

- Colons are also used to separate numbers, such as Bible chapters and verses, or hours, minutes and seconds when writing times.

  Examples: *John 3:14   School finishes at 2:45.*

Comma (,)

Commas are used to:

- Indicate where a reader should pause in a sentence.

  Example: *You expect me to help you, but you show little thanks in return.*

- Separate the person named or spoken to from the rest of the sentence.

  Example: *My teacher, Mrs Amos, is very kind.*

  Michael, have you finished your work yet?

- Separate words or phrases in a list. Two items are usually joined by 'and', eg *bows and arrows*. More than two items make a list and the items in a list are separated by commas.

  Examples: *We ate oranges, apples, pears and bananas.*

  I looked under the table, in the drawer, beside the desk and on the bench, but I couldn't find my pencil.

- In letter writing:

  After the salutation or greeting,

  Examples: *Dear Justin,   To whom it may concern,*

  At the conclusion, before signing your name.

  Examples: *Yours faithfully,   Best wishes,*

a b c d e f g h i j k l m n o **p** q r s t u v w x y z

- To separate direct speech from the rest of the sentence.

  Examples: *'You must keep moving,' said the police officer.*

  Mum yelled, 'Don't put that there.'

- To separate an embedded phrase, embedded clause or other 'asides' in a sentence. These are called parenthetic commas.

  Examples: *Ali, waving goodbye, stepped onto the bus.*

  The balloon, which was bright red, floated into the sky.

  Gina, my sister, is a very good golfer.

Dash (–)

- A single dash can be used when breaking off mid sentence for an abrupt change of thought.

  Example: *The next day we had better luck – but that's another story.*

- To signify missing letters or an interruption.

  Example: *'D— it!'   'Stop, or I'll –'   'You'll what?'*

- To emphasise or add information.

  Example: *These are bad laws – laws that need changing.*

- Dashes are used to show a range of numbers or values.

  Examples: *Chapters 2–6   June–July 1890–1921*

- Dashes can also be used to contrast or show a connection between two things.

  Examples: *Wallabies won 23–18   father–daughter dance*
  Sydney–Perth flight

Ellipsis (...)

An ellipsis indicates the deliberate omission of a word in a sentence. It can also be used to indicate a pause in speech, an unfinished thought, or, at the end of a sentence, to either heighten suspense, or indicate a trailing off into silence.

Examples: *And the winner is ...*

I haven't felt this tired since ...

- Ellipses may also be used to indicate missing words within quoted material.

  Example: *"Today we honour the Indigenous peoples of this land ... For the pain, suffering and hurt of these Stolen Generations ... we say sorry ..."* Kevin Rudd's Sorry speech 2008

Exclamation Mark (!)

- An exclamation mark is used after an expression of happiness, shock, surprise or dismay.

  Examples: *Hurray!*   *Oh no!*   *Wow!*

- Exclamation marks are used after short exclamatory sentences, which express strong feeling.

  Examples: *Good luck to you! What a surprise!*
  You poor thing!

Full Stop (.)

- A full stop is used at the end of a sentence that is a statement or command.

  Examples: *We rowed the boat across the stream.*
  Put it over here.

- Full stops can also be used after initials and in abbreviations, although it is becoming more common to omit the full stops.

  Examples: *Jane E. Brown, B.A.*   *U.S.A.*
  Meet me at 8.15 p.m.

Hyphen (-)

The hyphen is a small dash between word parts. It is used to show that the two words should be read as one word.

  Examples: *I drove down a one-way street.*
  The holiday deal was all-inclusive.

- Hyphens are also used when attaching some prefixes.

  Examples: *ex-wife   pre-owned   anti-aircraft*
  cross-reference

- A hyphen is also used when confusion may occur in a word.

  Examples: *reform / re-form   resign / re-sign*
  recreation / re-creation

- Hyphens are used in double-barrelled names and some titles.

  Examples: *Mary-Jo   John Barrington-Smith*
  sister-in-law   Editor-in-chief

- Compass points and numbers consisting of two words also use hyphens.

  Examples: *north-east   sixty-three   twenty-first*

Question Mark (?)

A question mark is used at the end of a direct question, or after a statement which is really a question.

Example: *Has that parcel arrived yet?*
            You really think you'll beat him?

- Tag questions are statements with a question tagged on the end.

    Example: *They went swimming, didn't they?*
               You will come to the party, won't you?

- A rhetorical question doesn't expect an answer, but does have a question mark.

    Example: *Who knew?   How hard could it be?*

- In direct speech, the question mark is placed inside the quotation marks, not at the end of the whole sentence.

    Example: *'Where are you going?' asked Dan.*

Quotation Marks ('' '' or ' ')

Quotation marks (also called inverted commas) are used to enclose the words that are actually spoken by someone.

Examples:

'I have just finished washing-up,' said Marvin.

Grandma whispered, 'I have a surprise for you!'

'Excuse me,' interrupted the minister, 'but I think you've taken the wrong book.'

Notice that the quotation marks always come after a comma or other punctuation mark at the end of conversation.

Quotation marks can also be used when quoting material from another source, when naming the title of a song, poem or TV show, and to draw attention to specific words in a sentence.

Examples:

Roald Dahl once wrote, 'A real witch gets the same pleasure from squelching a child as you get from eating a plateful of strawberries and thick cream'.

The little boy clapped his hands excitedly when 'Bob the Builder' came on the TV.

The word 'karaoke' comes from Japan.

Single marks ('… ') or double ones ("…") can be used, but whichever style you choose must be kept consistent within the one text. The exception to this rule is when you have a quote within quotation marks. In this instance, if you are using single quotation marks, you would put the internal quote in double, and vice versa.

Example: 'My favourite song is "Beat It" by Michael Jackson,' said Ronan. *(See also Direct Speech)*

Semicolon (;)

The semicolon marks a break in a sentence. It is a stronger pause than a comma.

It is used to:

- Link two independent clauses that express closely related ideas. Example: *Neither of us spoke; we simply waited.*
- Separate items in a list which contains internal punctuation.
  Example: *I met some interesting people: Ivan, a dentist; a mechanic called Bill; and Rosie, who is a ballerina.*
- Before linking words, such as *even so, so, therefore, for instance* and *nevertheless.*
  Example: *She took great care; even so, she made mistakes.*

PUNS

Puns are a humorous play on words which have similar sounds but different meanings. English is particularly rich in puns because it contains so many homonyms (words that are alike in sound or spelling, but different in meaning). Puns are most effective when spoken.

Examples: *'My jeans are ripped!'*   *'**Sew**, what's the worry?'*

Many puns in everyday conversation are not based on homophones or homonyms but rather on words that often have to be stretched or adapted to sound similar.

Example: *'My teacher has only one arm.'*
          *'Well, don't worry, he'd be pretty '**armless**.'*

Puns are often used in eye-catching newspaper headlines, and as attention-grabbing names for shops and restaurants.

Examples: Thai restaurants: *Thai Foon; Bow Thai*
Noodle bar: *Wok On In* Hairdresser: *Curl Up & Dye*

ROOT WORDS

The root of a word is the part of it common to all related words; the part from which they have all grown.

The main root words in modern English come from Old English, Latin or Greek.

Old English Roots

beatan (to strike), bat, battle, beat

beran (to carry), barrow, bear, berth, birth, brood, brother

bindan (to bind), band, bandage, bind

brecan (to break), brake, break, breakfast, brick, brittle

ceapian (to buy), cheap, chop

dragan (to drag), drag, bedraggled, draw, dray

faran (to go), far, fare, ferry, thoroughfare

fleotan (to float), afloat, fleet, float, flotsam

grafan (to dig), engrave, grave, groove, grove

stede (place), farmstead, homestead, instead, steady

Latin Roots

annus (year), anniversary, annual, biennial

brevis (short), abbreviate, brief, brevity

caput, capitis (head), cap, capital, captain

civis (citizen), city, civic, civil, civilian, civilisation

jacio (I throw), eject, objection, reject, inject

manus (hand), manual, manufacture, manuscript

mitto (I send), commission, missile, mission, transmit

pes (foot), biped, expedition, pedal, pedestrian, pedestal

primus (first), primary, primitive, prime

proprius (one's own), appropriate, proper, property, proprietor

The buttoned jacket we call a **cardigan** got its name from the fashion set by the Earl of Cardigan in around 1835.

Greek Roots

aster (star), asterisk, astrology, astronomy, disaster

autos (self), autocrat, autograph, automatic

bios (life), amphibious, biography, biology

demos (people), democracy, epidemic, demographic

dunamis (power), dynamic, dynamite

geo (earth), geography, geology

grapho (I write), autograph, geography

khronos (time), chronicle, synchronise

metron (a measure), diameter, metre, symmetry, metronome

polis (city), metropolis, policy, politics

skopeo (I see), microscope, scope, stethoscope, telescope

SENTENCES

A sentence is a group of words that makes sense and contains a verb. A sentence begins with a capital letter and ends with a full stop, question mark or exclamation mark.

There are four types of sentences.

- **Statements**, which simply state something or give information about something.

  Examples: *It is hot.   The time is eight o'clock.*
  Koalas are marsupials.

- **Questions**, which ask something.

  Examples: *What is the weather like?   Is it time to go?*
  Are koalas marsupials?

- **Commands** or requests, which direct someone to do something. They can also give advice or warnings.

  Examples: *Get out your books.   Sit up.*
  Look out for sharp stones.

- **Exclamations**, which express the strong feeling of the speaker or writer about something.

  Examples: *Look out!   I did it!   What a fun day!*

Sentences can take several forms.

Simple sentences consist of one clause. They can be divided into two parts; the subject, which tells who or what did something, and the predicate, which contains the verb and tells us what the subject did or is doing.

Examples: *Horses* (subject) *gallop* (predicate).

Billy (subject) *climbed the tree* (predicate).

Sometimes a sentence does not seem to have a subject.

Example: *Come here!*

In this case, even though the word is not actually said, the speaker is referring to you. The sentence is really saying:
(You) come here! The subject is understood.

Complex sentences have more than one verb and thus have more than one clause. A complex sentence has at least one **principal clause** (main clause) and one or more **subordinate clauses** (dependent clauses).

Example: *When I was ten, I went to hospital because I broke my arm.*

The **dahlia** flower was named after the Swedish botanist Anders Dahl, who introduced the plant into Europe from its native Mexico in the late 18th Century.

Compound sentences consist of two or more principal (main) clauses joined by a conjunction.

Example: *I washed the dishes and Billy dried them.*

SILENT LETTERS

The English language contains many words that have silent letters. These unsounded letters often confuse us when we try to spell such words. There are various historical (etymological) reasons for this. For example the word may have been pronounced differently in the past, with the silent letter sounded. For example, the **gh** in words such as *night* and *thought* was sounded in a rough guttural way, but over time it has been softened to say **f** as in *cough* or *enough*, or not heard at all. The silent **k** in *knife*, the **g** in *gnaw* and the **w** in *sword* were all once sounded.

We tend to skip over letters in words that are hard to pronounce, like the first **r** in *February* and *library*. Through common usage, one day they may become silent letters too.

Circle the silent letters in each of these words.

debt, castle, wriggle, soften, chemical, doubt, lamb, scissors, handsome, beret, knelt, depot, campaign, whole, drought

TRY THIS

SIMILES

A simile is a figure of speech that likens one thing to another.
Examples:

> as black as coal   as cold as ice
> as slippery as an eel   as fit as a fiddle
> as strong as an ox   as busy as a bee

Similes provide vivid word pictures of people and things. They often exaggerate the truth and add colour and interest to our language, both spoken and written.

SLANG

Slang is the use of informal words and expressions, which are not part of the standard language. People use slang for a number of reasons. Its novelty has strong appeal and it helps to introduce a friendly tone into a conversation or informal discussion.

Slang was once called *cant* and was the language used by thieves and villains in England.

The following are some Australian slang terms:

dodgy: something suspicious or underhand

beating around the bush: not getting to the point

panic merchant: someone who frequently overreacts

fair dinkum: genuine, true

a good lurk: on to a good thing or a good job

to stick your neck out: to take a risk

pull a swifty: to deceive or trick someone.

Popular rhyming slang includes:
tit for tat : hat, *trouble and strife* : wife, *froth and bubble:* trouble.

SPELLING

Spelling is the term we use for naming or writing the letters of a word in their correct order. Before printing was invented there were no standard rules for spelling. The word dictionary could be spelt in many ways:

dikshunary   diksionery   dictiunary   dickshunry

An American writer, Noah Webster, tried to introduce ideas to make the spelling of words easier. He believed all silent letters should be dropped, for example *debt* would become *det*.
He also suggested *colour* become *color*, *centre* become *center*, *axe* become *ax*, *plough* become *plow*.

Some of these changes can be seen in American English, however it is very difficult to change the spelling of words and changes occur very slowly. Today the word *hiccough* is sometimes spelled *hiccup*, the word *doughnut* spelled *donut* and even the word *through* sometimes is seen as *thru*.

Spelling Rules

Spelling rules are useful, however there are many exceptions so any rule must be treated with caution.

Some common rules or guides are:

- 'i' comes before 'e' except after 'c' when the sound is 'ee'. Examples: *receive, niece* and *ceiling*. One exception is *weird*.

- When a word ends in two consonants and we want to add a suffix such as 'ed' or 'ing' no letters are doubled. Example: *bang* becomes *banged* or *banging*.

- When a word ends in a consonant with a vowel before it, we double the last consonant before adding 'ed' or 'ing'. Examples: *stop, stopped; stab, stabbing*.

- When the word ends in 'y' it is usually changed to 'i' when a suffix is added. Example: *happy, happily; try, tried*. However, there are times when the 'y' is not changed – when 'ing' is added, for example, otherwise words like *crying* would become *criing*.

- When we add a prefix we do just that – add it! No spelling changes are necessary. Example: *un + necessary = unnecessary*.

- Drop 'e' before adding 'ing' and 'y'. Examples: *ride, riding; taste, tasty*.

- When a word ends in 'f', change the 'f' to 'v' before adding 'es', 'ed' or 'ing'. Examples: *wife, wives; half, halved; shelf, shelving*. One exception is *roof – roofs, roofing*. Also, words ending in 'ff' to not change.

Spelling Guide

- The vowels are **a, e, i, o, u**, and sometimes **y**. All other letters are consonants.

  'y' is a vowel in words such as *mystery*, but a consonant in words such as *yellow*.

- No word in our language ends in 'full' except the word *full* itself. All others are *ful*. Example: *beautiful*.

The word **sandwich** comes from the Earl of Sandwich, who was an avid card player. He hated having to leave the table to get something to eat so he made his servants bring meat between slices of bread.

- *Supersede* is the only English word ending in 'sede'.
- No English words end in 'v' or 'j'.
  (People's names are an exception, eg *Liv, Raj*.)
- The most common words we use that end in 'r' end in 'er'.
  Examples: *painter, teacher, tiger, scooter.* However, base words ending in 'ct', 'ate', 'it' and 'ey' usually end in 'or'. Examples: *escalator, doctor, editor, conveyor.* Base words ending in 'l' usually end in 'ar'. Examples: *pillar, similar, regular.*
- Most common words in English use the 'ise' ending.
  Examples: *surprise, advertise, organise.*
- *Prize* and *capsize* are the only two common words ending in 'ize'.
- *Analyse* and *paralyse* are the only two common words ending in 'yse'.
- There are only three 'ceed' verbs – *succeed, exceed, proceed.* All others use 'cede'. Examples: *precede, recede.*
- 'g' is usually a hard 'g' as in *grape, gallop, ignite.* However, it often says 'j' when followed by 'e', 'i' or 'y', particularly in word endings. Examples: *giant, gentle, gymnastics, tinge, changing.* There are exceptions. Examples: *give, get, geese.*
- 'c' in most cases says 'k' as in *catapult,* but when followed by 'e', 'i', or 'y', it says 's'. Examples: *city, cycle, fence.*
- 'q' is always followed by 'u'.
  Examples: *quiz, quick, equipment.*
  QANTAS is an acronym for Queensland and Northern Territory Air Service.
- When *well* and *all* are followed by other syllables, drop one 'l'. Examples: *welcome, also.*
- Words ending in 'ery' are usually obvious, as they have 'er' in the ending of the base word. Example: *baker, bakery.*
  In cases where it is not obvious, use 'ary'.
  Examples: *ordinary, dictionary, secretary.*
- Here is a rhyme to help your memory:
  'i' before 'e', except after 'c'.
  or when sounded like 'ay'
  as in *neighbour* and *weigh*.

Common Spelling Errors

The following is a list of frequently misspelt words, along with the reason for the incorrect spelling.

Words in which the wrong vowel is often used.

anchor	destroy	governor	regular	symptom
awful	different	impostor	sailor	system
business	divine	leisure	separate	tailor
cotton	doctor	persuade	similar	village
definite	figure	propeller	sugar	visible
deodorant	front	purchase	surface	

Words from which letters are often omitted.

address	descent	getting	opposite	stretching
admittance	difficulty	government	particular	success
afford	disappeared	guarantee	possession	suppose
ascend	disappoint	hottest	quarrelling	surprised
beautiful	dyeing	immediate	really	swimming
beginning	edge	jealous	receipt	traveller
biggest	eighth	library	referred	useful
carriage	except	marriage	safely	whiteness
changeable	February	misspelt	safety	woollen
committee	forgetting	occasion	science	
cupboard	fourth	occurred	shepherd	

Words in which letters are often added.

almost	balance	coming	shining	until
already	beautiful	film	skilful	using
always	beginning	fulfil	trespass	welcome
attached	burglar	hoping	truly	wooden
bachelor	buried	quarrelsome	umbrella	

SPOONERISMS

Reverend William Spooner was an educator and clergyman in England. He became famous for his creative and humorous mistakes while teaching at a college. Once, instead of saying the words 'conquering Kings', he said '*kinquering congs*'.

Reverend Spooner deliberately made these mistakes to make his sermons and lectures more interesting. Once he admonished a lazy student by stating: '*You have tasted two whole worms!*' What he meant, of course, was 'You have wasted two whole terms'. He was once alarmed when he saw a student '*fighting a liar*'. What he really meant was 'lighting a fire'.

Other sayings he is credited with include:

Let me sew you to your sheet. (Let me show you to your seat.)

You are occupewing my pie. (You are occupying my pew.)

Reverend Spooner's students themselves soon began inventing their own humorous mistakes, and called them *Spoonerisms*.

TRY THIS

Make up some humorous Spoonerisms of your own.

SUFFIXES

A suffix is a syllable added to the end of a word to change the part of speech.

Examples:

- *ist* meaning 'one who' can be added to *art* (a noun) to make *artist*
- *able* meaning 'capable of' can be added to *fashion* to make *fashionable*

Suffixes change words to another part of speech, so spelling changes are often needed.

Examples:

- *love* (a noun or verb) becomes *lovable* (an adjective)
- *history* (a noun) becomes *historical* (an adjective)

A suffix has a definite meaning which is usually derived from Old English, Latin or Greek.

Examples:

Old English Suffixes	Latin Suffixes	Greek Suffixes
craft (skill) – witchcraft	able (capable of) – movable	ic (belonging to) – frantic
er (comparative) – cheaper	ate (verb) – operate	y (abstract nouns) – melancholy
dom (power) – kingdom	al (belonging to) – loyal	ism (abstract noun) – atheism
est (superlative) – dearest	ee (denoting persons) – absentee	ics (sciences) – dynamics
en (diminutive) – kitten	ant (agent) – assistant	ise (to make) – characterise
ful (full of) – beautiful	ery (place) – bakery	ist (one who) – botanist
en (made of) – golden	ar (belonging to) – circular	
less (without) – luckless	ine (belonging to) – canine	

SYLLABLES

A syllable is a group of letters containing one sounded vowel only.

Examples: *free* (1 syllable)

trom bone = trombone (2 syllables)

lem on ade = lemonade (3 syllables)

dan ger ous ly = dangerously (4 syllables)

SYNONYMS

Synonyms are words that have the same or very similar meanings.

Examples: irate – *angry*, robust – *strong*, laundered – *washed*, repair – *mend*, conceal – *hide*, imitate – *copy*

In this list of synonyms the more difficult word is given first.

abandon	*leave*	annual	*yearly*	beverage	*drink*
abbreviate	*shorten*	anonymous	*nameless*	brief	*short*
abode	*dwelling*	anticipate	*expect*	catastrophe	*disaster*
abrupt	*sudden*	apparel	*clothes*	cautious	*careful*
abundant	*plentiful*	apparition	*ghost*	cease	*stop*
accommodation	*room*	arrogant	*haughty*	celebrated	*famous*
accurate	*correct*	assembly	*gathering*	centre	*middle*
adversity	*misfortune*	assistance	*help*	chivalrous	*gallant*
aggressive	*quarrelsome*	astonishment	*surprise*	circular	*round*
altitude	*height*	attired	*dressed*	coarse	*rough*
amiable	*friendly*	audacity	*impudence*	colossal	*huge*
ample	*plentiful*	austere	*severe*	commence	*begin*
animosity	*hatred*	avaricious	*greedy*	compel	*force*

comprehend	understand	gruesome	horrible	portion	part
conceal	hide	indolent	lazy	procure	obtain
conclusion	end	industrious	busy	prohibit	forbid
conversation	talk	infuriated	angry	prominent	outstanding
countenance	face	inquire	ask	prompt	quick
courageous	brave	insane	mad	puny	weak
courteous	polite	insolent	cheeky	purloin	steal
deceive	cheat	intention	purpose	putrid	rotten
deficiency	shortage	interior	inside	rare	scarce
demonstrate	show	intoxicated	drunk	reckless	rash
denounce	condemn	invaluable	priceless	recollect	remember
deride	mock	invincible	unbeatable	regret	sorrow
desert	forsake	jovial	jolly	reluctant	unwilling
despise	scorn	loathe	hate	reveal	show
detest	hate	lofty	high	robust	strong
diminish	lessen	lubricate	oil	ruddy	red
diminutive	small	mammoth	huge	scanty	scarce
disperse	scatter	margin	edge	sever	separate
drowsy	sleepy	mariner	sailor	significance	importance
dubious	doubtful	matrimony	marriage	slender	slim
edible	eatable	maximum	most	solitude	loneliness
elude	escape	mechanism	machinery	spectre	ghost
eminent	famous	melancholy	sad	squander	waste
encircle	surround	minimum	least	stationary	still
endeavour	attempt	moist	damp	sufficient	enough
energetic	active	motionless	still	summit	top
enormous	huge	mute	dumb	tempestuous	stormy
excavate	dig	necessity	need	tranquil	calm
exhibit	show	obstinate	stubborn	unite	join
extravagance	waste	odour	smell	vacant	empty
fatigue	weariness	omen	sign	valiant	brave
ferocious	fierce	option	choice	vanquish	conquer
frigid	cold	pandemonium	uproar	velocity	speed
generous	kind	pathetic	pitiful	wealthy	rich
glamorous	charming	peculiar	odd	wrath	anger
gleaming	shining	penetrate	pierce	wretched	miserable
gorgeous	splendid	perceive	see	youthful	young
gratitude	thankfulness	persuade	coax		
grave	serious	peruse	read		

TAUTOLOGY

A tautology is the unnecessary repetition of words or ideas.

In each of the examples below, both the italicised words and the bold words are saying the same thing; therefore, either could be omitted from the sentence.

He kicked three goals *himself* **personally**.

We *give these away* for **no charge**.

I helped her put all the counters in the centre of a *round* **circle**.

The twin boys are *exactly* **identical**.

The tyre rotated *round and round* **in circles**.

There are a lot of *unemployed* people who are **out of work**.

TEXTS

Texts deal with 'chunks' of language that are longer than sentences or paragraphs.

There are many different types of texts, which are determined by the **purpose** for which the text is written. In fact the entire structure of a text is determined by its purpose. When we look at the way in which a text is structured to achieve its purpose, we say we are studying its **genre** or **text type**.

Text Types

For more detailed information on Text Types and writing see Merryn Whitfield's, *Blake's Writer's Guide*.

There are three broad categories of text types:

- Imaginative (fiction)
- Informative (nonfiction)
- Persuasive (nonfiction)

Imaginative texts use made-up characters and/or events and often involve the reader in a personal response. They can also involve magical or 'impossible' ideas such as talking animals and travel through time.

Examples are *fairytales, anecdotes, picture books, novels, plays* and *poetry*.

Informative texts provide information in order to direct, inform or explain something to the reader. They usually try to be objective and not to take one side or point of view over another. Informative texts use real people and real events.

Examples are *recounts, reports, descriptions, explanations, biographies, news articles* and *procedures.*

Persuasive (or argumentative) texts attempt to persuade or to present two different sides to an issue. Their purpose is to make the reader think or act in a particular way. Persuasive texts use subjective language and opinion, not just facts.

Examples are *expositions, formal essays, letters to the editor, advertisements, reviews, interviews* and *discussions.*

THESAURUS

A thesaurus is a valuable tool for writers to use. It is a reference book like a dictionary that places words into groups according to their meanings. The group contains words of a similar meaning (synonyms) and words with opposite meaning (antonyms). A thesaurus is organised alphabetically to help you find the word or words you need.

So next time you are writing and looking for a more expressive word, consult your thesaurus.

TONGUE TWISTERS

Tongue twisters are groups of words deliberately arranged so that they are difficult to say, especially quickly. Many rely on **alliteration** for their effect.

Examples:

>Six thick thistle sticks.
>
>A swim well swum is a well swum swim.
>
>Ten tiny tooth tougheners.
>
>Double bubble gum doubles bubbles.

This one was one used as a sobriety test by police in the UK:

>The Leith police dismisseth us.

The most difficult tongue twister is claimed to be:

>The sixth sheik's sixth sheep is sick.

VERBS

Verbs consist of one or more words that tell us what is 'going on' in a sentence. They are an essential part of any written or verbal communication between people.

Types of Verbs

Action verbs are words that express a physical action. They are common in spoken language and in writing.

Examples: *work   run   sit   eat   jump*

More action verbs: *bounce, build, dawdle, fight, hurdle, kick, knock, meander, saunter, scatter, shatter, shuffle, squeeze, stagger, struggle, stumble, wriggle, bounce, protect, whistle, hurry, measure, poke, stretch, search, squeeze, scrub, arrive, leave, dance*

Saying verbs express a spoken action.

Examples: *talk   tell   said   suggest   yell*

More saying verbs: *yell, whisper, announce, define, exclaim, gossip, inform, instruct, swear, remark, wail, declare, convey, clarify, bellow, cheer, chuckle, giggle, growl, howl, joke, laugh, moan, shout, shriek, sigh, snarl, snigger, squeal, sob, cry*

Thinking and feeling verbs do not express a concrete action – they express actions that happen mentally, such as feelings, ideas, thoughts or attitudes. They are common in persuasive texts, narratives and some descriptions.

Examples: I **like** Sam.   I **think** people should recycle.
                   Katy **believed** the story. He **scared** the rabbit.

More thinking and feeling verbs: *believe, dislike, hate, feel, doubt, know, like, love, prefer, seem, suppose, think, understand, wonder, consider, enjoy, design, realise, reason, imagine, remember, satisfy, suffer, wonder, organise, detest*

Being and having verbs tell us about what things are and what they have. They are common in all kinds of descriptions.

Examples: Ben **is** a good swimmer. Ali **has** the answer.
                   They **are** here.

More being and having verbs: *am, are, is, was, were, be, being, been, has, have, had*

Is, are, has and *have* can also act as auxiliaries, or helping verbs, for doing, thinking and feeling verbs.

Example: Ben **is swimming**.

Verbs can be **finite** or **non-finite**.

- **Finite verbs** have a subject. For a sentence to be complete it must have a finite verb.

  Example: *The dog bit my leg.*

  The verb is *bit.* To find the subject of the sentence, ask 'Who or what *bit*?'. In this case there is an answer – *the dog* – so that is the subject.

- **Non-finite verbs** cannot stand alone. They can be **infinitives** or **participles**. Example: ***to go to*** the dance

The **infinitive** consists of a verb preceded by 'to'.

Examples: *to jump*   *to hop*

Often the **to** is not written or spoken.

Examples: *Fred made me* **do** *this.*   *Let me* **go** *with Sam.*

Participles are parts of verbs. When they are used with helping verbs (auxiliaries), they form compound verbs.

Example: *Jack* **is running** *across the lawn.*

The helping verb is *is* and the present participle is *running.*

Participles can be present or past. Examples:

Present   *swimming   skipping   hopping*

Past   *swum   skipped   hopped*

Note that a participle must never be used on its own as a verb.

Correct	**Incorrect**
I have done.	I done.
I have seen.	I seen.

Tense of Verbs

Verbs do not only express actions; they also tell us the time of the action. The tense of a verb tells us when the action is, was, or will be carried out.

The three tenses are past, present and future.

- **Present tense** refers to actions that are happening now, at this moment. Example: *I* **swim** *in the pool.*

- **Past tense** refers to actions that happened in the past; a few seconds ago or years ago. Example: *I* **swam** *in the pool.*

Don't confuse the past tense with the past participle. Remember, the past participle always has a helping verb.

Example: Past tense   *I rang.*

            Past participle   *I have rung.*

- Future tense refers to actions which will happen in the future; in a few seconds or in a few years.

    Example: *I **will swim** in the pool tomorrow.*

There are different forms of the present, past and future tenses.

- The examples above are in the **simple** form. They only have one part.
- The other main form is the **continuous** form. It refers to an action that is, was, or will be continuing.

    Present continuous tense   *He **is walking** along the road.*

    Past continuous tense   *He **was walking** along the road.*

    Future continuous tense   *He **will be walking** along the road.*

These are **compound** verbs – they have more than one part.

Most verbs form their tenses in a regular way according to the following table.

REGULAR VERBS

Present Tense	Past Tense	Present Participle	Past Participle
accept	accepted	is accepting	has accepted
believe	believed	is believing	has believed
climb	climbed	is climbing	has climbed
correct	corrected	is correcting	has corrected
cough	coughed	is coughing	has coughed
doze	dozed	is dozing	has dozed
finish	finished	is finishing	has finished
flood	flooded	is flooding	has flooded
jump	jumped	is jumping	has jumped
melt	melted	is melting	has melted
play	played	is playing	has played
pour	poured	is pouring	has poured
rub	rubbed	is rubbing	has rubbed
scrub	scrubbed	is scrubbing	has scrubbed
slice	sliced	is slicing	has sliced
sneeze	sneezed	is sneezing	has sneezed
snore	snored	is snoring	has snored
step	stepped	is stepping	has stepped
sway	swayed	is swaying	has swayed
toss	tossed	is tossing	has tossed
walk	walked	is walking	has walked

The **participle** is the part of the verb in a compound verb.
The auxiliary verb shows the tense.

Examples:

Present Tense	Past Tense	Present Participle	Past Participle	Future Tense
I *bake* a pie.	I *baked* a pie.	I *am baking* a pie.	I *have baked* a pie.	I *will bake* a pie.
He *talks*.	He *talked*.	He *is talking*.	He *has talked*.	He *will be talking*.

Irregular verbs do not add **ed** to form the past tense. The verb itself changes, and these changes have to be learned.

Examples:

IRREGULAR VERBS

Present Tense	Past Tense	Past Participle
Today I *drink*	Yesterday I *drank*	(I have) *drunk*
Today the water *freezes*	Yesterday the water *froze*	(It has) *frozen*
Today she *sweeps*	Yesterday she *swept*	(She has) *swept*
Today they *speak*	Yesterday they *spoke*	(They have) *spoken*

VOCABULARY

Vocabulary could best be described as the total stock of words used by a person or particular group or class of people.

There is actually a close bond between grammar of a functional or practical nature and breadth of vocabulary. For example it is easier for a student to understand the words *fraternity, fraternal, fraternise, fraternisation, fraternally, fratricide* if each is identified as a part of speech (eg noun, verb, adjective, adverb), each with a special function. Knowledge of the words will be even greater if we know that these words come from the Latin word *frater* meaning 'a brother'.

Word Meanings

To fully grasp the meaning of a sentence you have to understand the vocabulary. You must be aware of the meanings of each word and in what context it is being used.

Read these sentences:

Although she is an octogenarian, Sally is still the robust, garrulous lady she has always been.

Which word tells us Sally is still strong?

The following jumbled letters are said to be one of the hardest of all from which to make a word.

y o b n e a t

Do you know what the word is?

It has its origin from Bayonne in France where it was first made.

The word is bayonet which means 'a blade attached to a rifle'. It is difficult because we naturally expect the y to come last.

Michelle joined a quintet of actors.

Apart from Michelle how many other actors are in the group?

Consider the meanings of these sentences.

Can you determine their meanings from the vocabulary used?

- *I think a lot of you.   I think of you a lot.*

- *Jack brought the foul smelling dog home. Jack took the foul
  smelling dog home.*

Which one do you think Jack's parents would prefer?

- *Sally is a pretty, kind girl. Sally is a pretty kind girl.*

Which sentence do you think Sally would prefer?

VOICE

Active and Passive Voice

A verb can be in the active or the passive voice. The voice of
the verb tells whether the subject is doing the action (active
voice) or whether something is being done to the subject
(passive voice). When the passive voice is used, the verb
includes an auxiliary (helping verb) and a participle (main
verb).

Examples:

Active voice   *Katy read the book.*

Passive voice   *The book was read by Katy.*

Active voice is more direct, and usually shorter and easier to
read than passive voice. Passive voice is often used in reports
and explanations to neutralise events, and in public notices to
make them less hostile.

Examples:

Active voice   *Do not put your feet on the seats!*

Passive voice   *Feet must not be put on the seats.*

VOWELS

Vowels are the sounds produced when the air passes through the mouth without obstruction.

The vowels are **a, e, i, o** and **u**. Note: However, **y** sometimes does the work of a vowel, in words like *cry* and *fly* (sounding long 'i') or *mystery* (sounding short 'i'). In words such as *yellow* or *yeast* it is a consonant.

WORDS WE OFTEN MISUSE

There are certain words that are often misused in English. Study the following carefully and try to remember each.

amount   This should be used only for mass nouns but not count nouns. We say *a large amount* of work or sugar, but the number of mistakes, the number of horses etc.

beside   This means alongside and should not be confused with *besides* which means 'in addition to'.

*Sally stood **beside** the bed.*
*Did anyone else come **besides** you?*

between   We say something is shared *between* two people but *among* three or more.

*The teacher shared the lollies **between** Jim and Sally.*

*The teacher shared the lollies **among** all the students.*

both   This may not be used interchangeably with *each*. *Both* means two taken together. *Each* means any number taken one at a time.

***Both** these books cost a dollar.*
(Total cost is one dollar).

***Each** of these books cost a dollar.*
(Total cost of three books is three dollars.)

can   *Can* means being able to do something.
May means to have permission to do something.
Therefore if you want permission to read you say

May I read? but if you want to know if someone can play squash you say, ***Can*** *you play squash?*

disinterested A *disinterested* person is one who is impartial and is different to an *uninterested* person who lacks interest.

farther *Farther* means a greater distance. It should not be confused with *further* which means more or additional.

A ***further*** *point to consider is that she has travelled* ***farther*** *than us.*

fewer We use *fewer* for count nouns.

She has ***fewer*** *pencils than me.*

We use *less* for mass nouns.

She has ***less*** *sugar than me.*

hanged A painting can be *hung* on the wall, but a criminal is always *hanged*.

The prisoner will be ***hanged*** *tomorrow.*

learn *Learn* means to receive knowledge but *teach* means to convey knowledge.

I am going to ***learn*** *how to play golf.*

The coach will ***teach*** *me how to play golf.*

lie To *lie* means to recline while *lay* means to place or put something down. It always requires an object.

I ***lie*** *on the bed.*
(Note: Past tense of ***lie*** – I ***lay*** *on the bed.*)

Lay *the shovel on the ground.* (Note: Past tense of ***lay*** – I ***laid*** *the shovel on the ground.*)

principal The principal of a school is its leader. A *principle* is a rule of conduct. Don't confuse these words. Remember the **principal** is your pal.

unique This word means the only one that exists. We must never say *more unique* or *most unique*.

The words
cauliflower
and education
contain all the
vowels.
Look through
a dictionary
and find some
more.

page 3

LPG, kg, GBH, EST, eg

page 4

Berrigan – rose bush scrub;
Dunedoo – swan;
Omeo – mountains/hills;
Maralinga – fields of thunder;
Murrumba – good place;
Dungog – a clean hill;
Echuca – meeting of the waters;
Popanyinning – water hole

ANZAC – Australian & New Zealand Army Corps;
NASA – National Aeronautics & Space Administration;
ATM – Automatic Teller Machine;
RADAR – Radio Detection and Ranging;
ALCOA – Aluminum Company of America;
AIDS – Acquired Immunodeficiency Syndrome

page 14

dray, dress, drill, drunk, drying; flack, flick, flimsy, flock, flush

page 15

centre, theatre, axe, pyjamas, traveller

diaper – nappy; schedule – timetable; sidewalk – footpath/pavement; closet – wardrobe; trunk – car boot; baby carriage – pram; soda – soft drink; busboy – junior waiter; trash – garbage/rubbish; cracker – savoury biscuit; robe – dressing gown; pocketbook – handbag; candy – chocolate; druggist – chemist

page 16

softer – foster/forest; marble – ramble; melon – lemon; heart – earth; spear – spare/pears; luster – result/rustle; disease – seaside; battle – tablet; untied – united; sprite – stripe/priest/ripest; danger – angered/garden/gander/ranged

lion : pride, whale : calf, Tokyo : Japan, water : drought

page 17

lost – found; child – adult; true – false; war – peace; clean – dirty; black – white; left – right; correct – wrong

page 19

galah – a pink and grey cockatoo; also slang for a silly person; goanna – a large lizard; chuck a u-ey – to do a u-turn (changing direction) when driving; damper – a traditional Australian bread, usually made over a campfire; drongo – slang for a stupid person; also the name of a bird; lagerphone – an Australian 'bush' instrument made from metal bottle tops nailed loosely onto a broom handle, which rattles when banged; whinger – someone who complains a lot; wowser – a prudish person, or spoilsport; yabby – a small freshwater crayfish;

mulga – a variety of acacia tree; paddock – a field for grazing livestock; kelpie – an Australian sheep dog; joey – a baby kangaroo; jackeroo – a hired farm hand who rounds up livestock on horseback; g'day – informal greeting, abbreviation of 'good day'; bloke – slang for a man; dunny – slang for toilet

page 25

b) a bit steep – far too expensive; a smack in the eye – very discouraging, an insult; to take it lying down – not to offer any resistance; to peter out – to come to an end; to take the rap – to take the blame for someone else; to get the boot – to be tossed out or fired; for all he was worth – to his maximum capacity

page 49

a) NEI **b)** NEI **c)** F **d)** T **e)** I

page 51

The wind was a torrent of darkness; The moon was a ghostly galleon; The road was a ribbon of moonlight

page 85

de**b**t, cas**t**le, **w**riggle, sof**t**en, **ch**emical, dou**b**t, lam**b**, **sc**issors, hand**s**ome, beret, **k**nelt, depo**t**, campai**g**n, **wh**ole, drough**t**